Bag of Bricks

MICHAEL DUBÉ

Library and Archives Canada Cataloguing in Publication

CIP data on file with the National Library and Archives

ISBN 978-1-926582-70-2

INTRODUCTION

In the midst of a physical and mental breakdown, I managed to sit at my old computer and pound out the story of my life, choosing to reveal my most kept secrets as they related to my present situation. Needless to say (breakdown) my present situation was not a good one.

I'm not certain what compelled me to write this book. Certainly its subject matter is far from unique. I believe my effort came from a need to tell myself my own story. To get it all straight in my own mind. It was the only way I knew how to sort through the mess, in hopes of making any sense of it.

Little did I realize at the time, that these pages would not only help me to understand, or better understand, the turning upside-down of my existence, but would also serve to educate my children as to what happened to our family.

I learned from this story, though I must admit that not all that I learned was good. I healed some from this story, and I hope my children did as well. In writing this book, I hope my children, and my siblings, learn more about me.

I hope you take something away from my story that makes you a better person, a more understanding person, more accepting, more humble, more loving.

Michael.

Acknowledgements

First, I want to thank the academy… Oh that's old.
Seriously, all my love and thanks go out to the following people:
I need to thank everyone who helped me through my personal nightmare. **Mom**, **Bev**, **Deb,** and **Bi**, our trip up north for Granny's un-funeral, sadly, couldn't have come at a better time. That was the most fun I'd had in ages, and since. We really should do another road trip. Love you guys immeasurably.

Christopher Duliban, you've been my backbone, well, at least a couple of discs. I know you know how I feel about you, but I'll tell you again anyway. You're my brother, man. You must be part of my life from now on, no matter what. And those who'd rather cut you from their lives are at a great loss. You know that.

Speaking of brothers, **Dwayne Trembley** of Delhi, ON, without knowing you I can't imagine what life would have been like. You made the difference. Always love you, bro.

Taylor, Randee, Hunter, and **Chanel**, my four fantastic children, who proved to me that good can overcome evil. Hehehe. I love my brats so f*!#ing much! Endless love, guys, well, guy and girls.

Dr. Paulo Oliverio: My only Italian brother. I'm proud of you like you're my own son. Your heart is like the Grinch's after it grew! I've never met a more caring soul. Thank you for everything.

Dr. Liam: There will never be another man in my life like you. Maybe someday I'll fall in love, but you'll always be first in my heart. Love you always, Liam, always.

PART 1 * 2008

Under The Sheets With A Cousin

I was born on October 27 1968, (*I was born*, always a good way to begin a tell all book, I guess), the fifth addition to the four children Paul and Jeanne were raising (well, Mom was raising) on a small farm in little known Port Robinson, Ontario, Canada. Mom handled the farm chores and the caring of us kids, while Dad made a living driving his own dump truck. I've heard all the growing up stories from my sisters about their years on that farm. Like the chicken that ran into the forest after Dad cut its head off, never to be seen again. The miscarriage Mom had. The cross-country hike my brother and sisters took to a nearby airport, without parental permission, and the straps they received upon returning home that evening.

We sold the farm and moved into a restaurant in Port Colborne. Again, there are the stories from my siblings, such as the one about some neighborhood kid named Pooper; whether that was his nickname or his real name, no one knows. Apparently, the little shit shoved me off of our roof as Beverly and Debbie watched helplessly from the kitchen window. Despite having heard the story a million times, I myself was still too young to remember.

My lifelong task of memory collecting began for me at about age four. We were then living on Elgin Street in Welland, in a large duplex my father owned. I remember watching my parents pull into our driveway as I stood anxiously awaiting my mother's return from the hospital. She had tears streaming down her rosy cheeks, and in her arms, wrapped in a pink fleece blanket, was the newest and final aggravation—uh—addition to our family.

Four years after me, the five of us became six: Richard, Beverly, Debbie, Tammy, Me, and Bibianne—named after my father's mother. We've long since dropped the 'Bibianne' to Bianne and then to Bi. It's pronounced *BeeBeeAnne.* Not ByeByeAnne, and not Bye—Bee! Just thought I'd clear that up for her sake.

We were quite *The Brady Bunch.* We didn't have much in the way of riches, but poor was not a familiar term to me in those days. Everyone lived pretty much within the same means as we did (it was the times). We had a big floor-model television to watch black and white programs. The changing knob was broken off so we used pliers to change channels. It was a sizable house, which sufficiently accommodated our bunch. My mother was a stay-at-home mom and my father bought and sold houses for a living. It's what she always did, and it's what he always did.

Winters were good. We went skating and tobogganing at Chippawa Park; lot of great memories from that park. As Christmas approached, we all went caroling to earn some cash to buy gifts for our parents. People were generous back then. Kids would never go caroling nowadays. Do they even know what caroling is? Guess it's for the best; they'd probably be shot, nabbed, robbed, or worse. Yeah, winters were good, but summers were even better.

My father had picked up an old school bus and turned it into our traveling home on wheels. My mother sewed matching curtains and cushions for the many windows and seats. That bus was equipped with a fridge, stove, cupboards, washroom, dining table, four bunk beds at the rear, and one bed where my brother slept at the very back. The table became a double bed and the one sofa became a bed at the front of the bus. Plus, one more smaller sofa was used for sleeping on as well.

In its early days our bus (or Nellie, as my father named her) was quite a unique camper. My brother and sisters had painted cartoon character on both sides of her, above the windows, in square sections. Her main colors were red and white, and my father had mounted a set of Texas bull horns on the hood. Okay, the horns were a bit garish, but we were so proud of that camper. She ran like shit but we always managed to get to where we were going.

Even rode that bitch to Florida one summer. For the most part, her journeys began in Welland and ended up north at our relatives' in Smooth Rock Falls.

The drive there was like riding a bus to camp. We'd sing the same songs every time, munch on junk food, busy ourselves with coloring books, and even celebrated Debbie's birthday with a cake one time. And when we saw the statue of a polar bear, we knew we'd arrived.

Our cousins were another family with six children. There was someone for everyone. I was fortunate enough to be somewhere in the middle of my cousin Mark and his younger sister, Sadie, which meant I had two playmates. However, I only spoke English while my cousins only spoke French, except the 'F' word—we all knew how to say that. Despite the language barrier, we somehow managed to understand one another. Most of the time, I was able to follow what they meant by their changing tones and hand signals. I never understood them word for word.

Their family lived in a small house, with their father's lumber business next door. They also owned a splendid cottage at nearby Departure Lake. Once we arrived, we all headed to the cottage, where we would spend most of our vacation. That cottage had everything from an old wood stove that we used to flat-iron loaves of bread into crispy paper-thin toast, to a television (rare in those days). Man, we had awesome times up there.

When we weren't at the cottage, we found ways to occupy ourselves around their house. I remember us kids piling into my uncle's pickup at night to head into their puny town for sodas. And during the day, I played up in Mark's tree-house, rode double on his rickety old bicycle, picked blueberries, made frequent treks through his father's shop, and sometimes ventured off for a swim at the local pool. I'll never forget that one afternoon, while standing in line to get into the pool, I met a kid who had his ear pierced. If you know anything about the times (1970s), then you know he was way ahead of 'them,' as far as fashion goes.

My uncle's house was always filled with laughter. As minuscule as their kitchen was, we all gathered there for dinners and endless conversations. On nights when the drop in temperature made sleeping in our bus impossible, we shared in the warmth of our cousins' beds. Though it didn't seem like it then, their bedrooms were pocket-sized. And one summer, while sharing in the coziness of Mark's bed with him, he took it upon himself to introduce me to something he'd learned, from whom, I never knew.

There in the dark, the radiator hissing, the two of us lying on our backs next to each other, he reached down into my pajamas and tenderly wrapped his fingers around my penis. What Mark did next would cause my little toes to curl and my buttocks to squeeze together. Masterfully skilled, he began to roll his fingers up and down around my penis's head. The sensation was incredible. His thumb and forefinger pressed and rubbed. I'd never known I could feel anything like that...***there***! Mark's arousing manipulations were nothing less than genius. He continued for a while, until I was getting sleepy. At one point he was going to stop but I pleaded with him to continue. I was an instant addict.

The following night, of course, I asked him to do that ***thing*** again. He did. I don't know how many nights he did it. I never told anyone, and that's probably when my first real secret was born. I didn't think of the act as being anything dirty; after all, in the morning we were still just two boys. Funny part is, I never asked him to show me exactly what it was he was doing that gave me such pleasure. And so, I didn't learn how to recreate those titillating vibrations for myself (well, not at that point in time).

Elgin Street

I LEARNED HOW TO RIDE a two-wheeler on Elgin Street. On a brand new (secondhand) yellow bike my father picked up. I learned how to play 'You show me yours, I'll show you mine,' with the neighbor's daughter on the swing on our front porch, under a blanket (it was her idea!) I learned how cruel the kids down the street could be, when they shouted names like 'bedbugs, bedbugs!' at us. But for the most part, I liked living on Elgin Street.

Once I was inside that house I felt safeguarded from the world's prying eyes. I could play séance with Bev, Debbie, and Tammy. Help them build Frankenstein's monster out of Dad's clothes on the basement freezer, only to scare ourselves silly with it afterward. And I could play Barbies with Tammy (that's what we called it, 'Playing Barbies). Tammy liked to play 'dirty' with her dolls, pretending Ken and Barbie were making out. She was a little pervert. I'd like to know where the influence was coming from. They certainly weren't showing stuff like that on *Family Affair*.

Not having money to buy many toys, my mother used to let us cut the models out of the Sears Catalog to play with. We'd even cut out the babies so our family's could have kids. I found myself looking through the pages with the male models more than the woman's bra section (something I still do to this day). Those catalogs were my first real connection to the male world. I could look at those photographs all I wanted and no one knew, no one cared.

Elgin saw Richard get his first drum kit and learn how to play "Wipe Out." We used to love watching him play, watching him show off to us. One of his friends became Bev's boyfriend, and my first crush. I was young enough that Bev used to make me give her boyfriend a kiss on the cheek before I went up to bed at night. That guy had the bluest eyes and curly blond hair. He was really hot then. I know what he looks like now and believe me—Yuk! I was probably about four or five years old, but I still remember how I liked to sit on his lap. Guess Bev was lucky I wasn't old enough to steal her man. Knowing what I know now about him, I was lucky, too.

I started grade school on Elgin Street, attending St. Kevin's Catholic School. It was several blocks from our house. One incident, which has nothing to do with sexuality—or does it?—stands out in my mind. Sitting on the classroom floor, surrounding the teacher during reading time (a half hour when she'd read to us from some book) I was afraid to raise my hand and tell her I had to go pee. So I didn't tell her, but I still went pee. No one in class noticed the wet spot, but when I got home my sister Debbie did. She ratted me out to my mother. Debbie was, and still is, the great and wonderful tattle-tale in my family. I'm sure my other sisters would back me up on that one. Anyway, my brilliant explanation for the wet pants was that there was this *BIG* puddle on the way home and… I was a born story teller.

The next year, in grade one, I found myself with two girlfriends: Selene and Carry. They were friends already and opposite personalities in every way. Selene was the pretty little blond, who knew she was a pretty little blond. And Carry—sorry Carry—was the not-so-attractive but fun girl. I preferred Carry's company to that of Selene's. I remember pretending that we were taking a shower together in her backyard, Selene and me (her idea!) I don't think I ever played any such games with Carry. Carry was a buddy. I never kissed those girls. Maybe we were too young. (No, that's not it.) Maybe I had no yearning to. (Yeah, that's it.) I don't recall how the three of us drifted apart. My guess is that the introduction of a boy in my life probably drew my attention away from them. Boys will play with girls, but they always go back to their friends of the same gender.

THE SILVER DOLLAR

I WAS WELL INTO GRADE TWO when my family packed up and moved from Elgin Street. It was an exciting time (for me, at least). We landed on the opposite side of Welland, on Ontario Road. Our new home was a house/restaurant/store combo. The name of our restaurant was The Silver Dollar. My father had a giant-sized Canadian silver dollar mounted on the front of the restaurant. It was pretty cool, I thought.

Tammy and I were the only ones still going to St. Kevin's. We had to ride a taxi there and back. It was all so glamorous to us, being chaperoned to and from school. Every day our lunch consisted of a healthy bag of chips, a chocolate bar, some cake snack, and usually a can of soda. I usually traded my friend Matt my bag of sour cream n' onion chips for his tuna sandwich. I feel sorry for Matt's mother: all those tasty tuna sandwiches she made for her son that kept me well fed.

Life was chaotic for my brother and sisters, and my poor mother. Dad made Richard, Bev, and Debbie run the restaurant and store. He even forced Bev to quit her real job to come and work for him—without pay! They went through hell in that place, serving up meals for the local riff-raff. And me, I met two new girls to call girlfriends. They had different names and different faces but it was Selene and Carry all over again.

Judy lived in the small house right next to our restaurant. She had straight blond hair, brown eyes, and a tall, slim physique. Her two older sisters both had the hots for Richard. He even dated the eldest sister for a while. They were all blonds. I hung with Judy for the same reason I hung with Selene—I candy. She wasn't very fun to be with. No real sense of humor. I didn't do much with her, other than the odd kiss now and then.

Now Carla, on the other hand, was another Carry. Carla lived a few blocks from us. She was a bit on the plump side but I thought she was prettier than Judy. I went many places with Carla. She was fun and normal. She wasn't stuck-up like Judy. Carla and I would hold hands when we walked to the park. I'd even help her baby-sit once in a while. There's still a soft spot in my heart for Carla. She was sincere. If you're going to have a childhood sweetheart, have a Carla.

I had a cousin living across the street from us. He was several years older than I. He wasn't one of my favorite people to play with. He had some nifty Tonka trucks, but Freddie seemed to have trouble staying focused. We'd start to play and next thing I knew, he was throwing frogs into the air to knock them out. Then he would place the frogs under the tires of his father's pickup. Freddie would put the truck in neutral and really get his rocks off on squishing frogs.

I don't recall ever going to the park with him or even leaving his yard with him. I doubt he was allowed to, and I'm sure the other neighbors were thankful for that. His mother was an obese woman. She always seemed to be calling out to Freddie in her squeaky, annoying voice. "Fredieee," she'd drawl. He was always in trouble for something. Not unlike the red-headed boy who lived across from another cousin's house, behind us.

I only spent one afternoon with Tom's friend. His life was hell. His father was abusive to him. This kid was so different to me. I admired him, even though the abusive father. I found him attractive. His eyes, his legs, his feet in his funny sandals, and most of all—his sadness. (Now how weird is that?) Tom and I convinced that poor kid to come with us to the nearby swimming pool. I remember wishing it was just him and I that day, and not Tom.

By the time we returned to Tom's street the kid's father had returned. From the end of the kid's driveway, where his father yelled at us to go home, Tom and I watched in disbelief as our friend's arms and back met with several lashings from his father's angry leather belt. It was intense. The pair disappeared into their house, and I never saw that kid again.

The one thing I was *not* while living at The Silver Dollar was lonely. When Tom and Freddie were off doing something together, being closer to each other in age than I was to them; and girlfriends became monotonous, I played with another kid down the street. Oddly enough, I could never remember his name, but I never forgot his older sister's. (And hers not being important, I'll call him Alex.)

Now that I think about it, he and his sister probably didn't live on my street at all. The house we played behind was most likely their grandparent's house, or something. I'm concluding this because I didn't see them often. Playing with Alex was more like a two or three time deal. And I'm sure he would have come over a lot more had he actually been living there. It makes sense.

Okay. So I've established that Alex only visited my street, but when he did, we were bad boys. We were little piglets. Behind my house there was a huge ditch, where we saw many rats foraging about. My father had a dumpy camper back there (yeah, you know where I'm going with this). When we were sure that no one else was around, Alex and I went to play in that trailer. I don't know whose idea it was, but we took turns putting our penis's in each other's mouths. I remember vaguely that his tasted and smelled of pee. And though we were careful to be quick about the exchange, it wasn't the last time we would experiment.

When we played touch-tag in his backyard with his sister and some other kids, I remember thinking that I'd just assume drop the game and return with him to the trailer. We never did anything more than sample each other, and I can't say it was pleasurable in the slightest. So why did we keep trying? Because it was a natural curiosity? Because monkeys do it? Because it was in us to seek one another out for a pleasure we barely understood? I didn't know the answers then. I'm sure he didn't either. I didn't think about the reasons why, only the need to try more. Like the incident with cousin Mark, it was just another thing that happened, and there was no repercussion.

I'm not certain just how long we lived at The Silver Dollar, but we moved back across town to the St. Kevin's area. I'm sure my older siblings were ecstatic. Our house on Carlton Avenue was unique to me. The living room was on the second floor, along with a small kitchen, washroom, and a couple of bedrooms. The main floor became Richard's bedroom and the laundry room. My room upstairs was pretty small but I liked it. Mom gave me my very first portable record-player for Christmas in that house, with my two very first record albums: Ricky Nelson's "Greatest Hits," and a Diana Trask album with the song "Teddy Bear" on it.

The Silver Dollar hadn't sold, but a few months later, the building conveniently burned down. We ended up having boxes and boxes of candy and chips brought to our new house. The smell of smoke was on everything. (Here's where you cock an eyebrow.) Seems everywhere my father's been, a trail of mysteriously burned buildings lye in his wake. The restaurant we owned in Port Colborne also met an untimely death at the hands of pyromaniacs. The Silver Dollar was death by fire number two. Hhmm. Very suspicious. Then came the flaming ends to several buildings he owned but couldn't sell in Crystal Beach. And still another restaurant of his crumbled to ashes up north as well. (Did I just out my father as an insurance scammer?)

Getting back to Carlton, I immediately became friends with the boy next door, Rocco. Rocco had a habit of mouthing whatever words he'd just spoken. He lived with his single mother and three sisters. Tammy chummed around with the two older sisters like they were *Charlie's Angels*. The littlest sister, unfortunately for her, was the ugliest kid I'd ever seen.

Rocco was one of those kids who pretty much ran his own life at such an age. I rarely saw his mother. He used to sneak into a nearby Canadian Tire store and look under their counters for fallen change. A few times he even found bills under there. I was soon overlooking the embarrassment of the act to search myself. I truly enjoyed playing with Rocco. Finally another boy who was into playing *Godzilla* and *The Bionic Man*, and who was more comfortable with his sexuality than any other boy I'd ever known.

Our dicks pretty much looked the same, Rocco's and mine. We never did any touchy feely stuff (he wasn't that kind of boy), but he had no qualms about running around the house naked, even in front of his little sister. We once took a bath together, but he wasn't looking at me the way I was looking at him. Rocco was like my brother in that sense: Richard had no hang-ups about his nudity, either. I guess you don't have to be self-conscious when there's no chance you'll pop-a-boner in front of other guys.

Our days on Carlton were short-lived. Following the blizzard of '77, Dad came up with this clever plan to move to Florida. Having his duel citizenship would have made our becoming American citizens easy. None of us were happy with this plan. We'd only just settled in. Alas, Dad's cowboy-boot-wearing foot was down—we were moving.

We had to have a big yard-sale. I remember that sale quite clearly because Bev and Mom had to argue with Dad to let me keep a picture of a sad-eyed puppy. It was just a picture, for Pete's sake. Thankfully, Mom and Bev won the argument on my behalf because when we moved it wasn't to Florida. I would have sacrificed my puppy picture for nothing. After a mere two weeks in grade four, we moved to Wallace Avenue, taking over my grandparents old house.

Who Ordered The Bullies?

St. Andrew's wasn't a bad school. My second day there I went on a class trip to Niagara Falls to collect fall leaves. The students were mostly Italian. I had the upper hand when it came to French class, except that I was often overlooked because of my French background. My grade four teacher was Mrs. Lasovich. She was pretty sweet on me because I was such a polite and quiet student (and I was cute, too). I remember she asked me permission to keep one of my drawings from Art class. I was very good at Art. The picture was of a Horned Owl. I really liked it but I let her keep it anyway.

(In 1976, back at St.Kevin's School, I won first prize for an Art contest that all the Welland schools were involved in. The subject was physical fitness. I drew a person running through their backyard, with a house, a tree, and of course, the sun in the upper right-hand corner. I rocked that contest. Later, in grade eleven, I received another award for Art. This time I was 'Best Grade Eleven Boy' in Art. My Art teacher, Mr. Furgison, included ten bucks in an envelope for me—he was sweet on me, too. I was still cute!)

Our first year living on Wallace was okay, I guess. If you don't include the bullies I had to deal with on a daily basis. Two boys who attended the public school across the street from our house made it part of their morning ritual to spit at me, kick me as they rode past on their bicycles, and pretty much make my walk down our street a nightmare. Why? Who the hell knows?

My older sister, Tammy, walked with me. She yelled at them everyday in my defense. I never said anything; I didn't want to provoke them with a response (as if they needed provoking). I usually hid on the other side of Tammy as they rode by. One kid was pretty tall and over-weight. The other was taller than I, but smaller than his partner in crime. Their bullying went on for about half the year.

Meanwhile, I had another bully to deal with. This one went to *my* school and lived on the corner of *my* street! His name (not really) was Bob. Bob got into fights every...single...day at school, and usually with the same kid. His enemy was about the same size and shape as he was, and lived to the right of my house! Both these boys were troubled kids, and both were double my size. (Let's call this other kid James.)

So there I was in the middle of these two morons. Bob insisted on chasing me home from school, never once able to catch me. I was a good runner and he had water on his knees—seriously. When I wasn't running from Bob, I was walking James home, being his shoulder to cry on sortaspeak. He was a nice kid. If not for Bob, he probably wouldn't have been in trouble at all. And just like myself, he had no idea why Bob was after him. I couldn't believe that I was actually a friend to this tough blond-haired kid who could kick my ass.

Finally, on the day that ended my attacks from the public school kids, Tammy and I had just reached the corner of our street. The shorter bully, without his hefty partner, came running across the intersection to get me. "I'm sick of your shit!" he said, as if I'd ever done anything to him. As he tried to hit me, I ran circles around the mailbox. He eventually was able to hit me on the head a few times, while I covered myself with my hands.

Tammy then jumped in, yelling, "Leave him alone, you asshole!" She booted that little prick right in the ass. She was awesome. No one could bully Tammy, even to this day.

And then, through friends we'd met, we began to take a new route to school. It was quicker and it allowed me to avoid the bullies. And somehow, I don't know how, but Bob became my friend. There were many times when he'd ask me why he had been after me in the first place. One time I flat out told him, "Because you're an asshole." James moved away shortly thereafter. But that didn't stop Bob from being called down to the school office everyday. And as he and I became closer friends, I learned he wasn't as tough as he wanted people to believe he was.

Grade four was a difficult year for me. You might call it my year of the bullies. Being the quiet type, I didn't approach anyone in my new class to make friends with. But eventually a nerdy blond-haired kid with tiny round spectacles introduced himself to me. He was a little shorter than everyone else and quite a bit brainier. A real favorite of the male teachers for some reason. Our school was located about ten feet from the Church of the same name, where 'Tweedy, or Bird,' as the teachers nicknamed him, was a choirboy. I soon learned the reason behind his nickname: Ralf was fascinated with birds, always carrying books on birds around with him. A total nerd.

But when I accepted Ralf's friendship, I also got his only friend, Andy's, friendship. Andy was kind of nerdy too. He never wore anything but cotton plaid shirts. His glasses were large and too big for his face, I thought. But he and I were a lot alike. Yeah, I admit it: I was nerdy. The two of us eventually became better friends than he'd been with Ralf. I bet Ralf regretted introducing himself to me after that, though he never *squawked* about it.

I think instead, Ralf made subtle attempts to win me over. We played handball a few times after school. I even helped him deliver his flyers up and down my street...once. Ralf took piano lessons, which I thought was also kind of nerdy at the time. He lived in a small house with two older brothers and his parents. His mother's voice on the phone was so soft and precious, yet when you met her, she wasn't so soft. I liked his father—big surprise. He was a nice, good-looking man. Ralf's parents eventually split up, leaving Ralf pretty bitter toward his old man.

Any time the students were asked to pair up, Andy and I were quick to choose each other. I think Ralf used to pair up with Nick, another straight-A student whose obesity made him a prime target for the jerks in our class. I personally never made fun of Nick, but his repulsive odor did gross me out. He was constantly pulling his pants out of his ass-crack. Nick played the accordion—need I say more?

Andy and I were both lousy at Mathematics. I would go to his house to do our homework, so we were sure to both get the answers wrong. He lived an only child with his parents. His mother was several years older than his father. They were really nice people. I practically lived at their house.

Andy had had an older brother whom I learned died from a disease. Andy inherited all of his brother's belongings. I was told his brother had once played drums on *Tiny Talent Time*, a Canadian program which showcased kids and their talents. If his parents were ever sad about the loss of their son, I never saw it. Andy and I were no trouble around the house. We were both quiet types. I think we spent most of our time listening and recording songs off the radio, on his brother's old stereo.

Both Andy and I changed in the stalls for gym class at school, partly because the washroom was so damn small, and partly due to shyness. We both hated phys ed. I hated everything about gym class: baseball, basketball, volleyball, floor hockey, track and field, square-dancing, and dodge ball! I just wasn't good at playing games. I didn't want to get hurt. I had bullies for that, remember? Okay, so I just hated sports: hated playing it, hated watching it, hated *it*. To me, there was nothing worse than gym class, other than Math. And to make matters worse, I had the same asshole teacher for both classes.

But things weren't all bad outside of school. Bob had since introduced me to the little guy who lived in the distance between his house and mine. Devon was thee smallest kid I'd ever met. He suffered from Polio, so his legs were underdeveloped, causing him to walk rather penguin-like. I can only imagine what hell he must have gone through prior to our meeting. Devon's parents called him Peanut, so his brothers called him Penis. And just as Ralf's introducing me to Andy had shifted the friendship ties, so did Bob's introduction to Devon.

Devon and I really hit it off. He and his family were quite different from any other families I'd ever known. They cussed a lot—all of them. Devon, his older brother Kenny, and I would hide behind their front porch railing and encourage their three-year-old niece to call out names to male passersby. Names like Faggot and

Queer and Asshole. Faggot was a really popular name we used back then. We even made up sayings like: Bite the bag, Fag; and Suck the weenie, Houdini.

When darkness fell, we'd gather a few other kids on our street and play hide and seek. There was a brother and sister at the corner in an apartment across from Bob's house. They lived there with their tramp mother. She once answered our knocks at her door wearing nothing more than a skimpy towel. Oh, yeah, she was definitely a slut. Lynn and Don were good kids in spite of their mother. Don rarely had time for playing; he went around cutting grass to earn money and did other odd jobs. I didn't see him as a happy child. His sister, whom I had a crush on, wasn't often allowed out to play. We really didn't see them much.

Devon and his brother could be found playing street hockey most days. Since I didn't play hockey, Devon and I often pretended we were the Globe Trotters in his driveway. And when we weren't famous basketball players, we played a pretty good game of marbles against neighborhood kids. I won a lot of marbles and learned their different names. Bob once accused me of donning a purse, when in actuality, he'd seen me with my alley bag. Yeah, once a bully, always a goof. He even stole a coin from my bedroom once. Bob made stealing a habit, one he'd be caught for while I was at his side. He and I lost touch, only hanging out together occasionally, such as when Devon and I would go skateboarding with him, and that was a rare event.

Backyard Camping

THAT FIRST SUMMER on Wallace proved to be very exciting for me, and troubling. While I was living my kid life, things were changing at home. Richard had moved into his own little house a few streets from us. It was a hippie house. His toilet sat in the corner of his kitchen, right out in the open. Each end of his ragged sofa was pressed snuggly against the paneled walls of his miniature living room. He'd hung his wolf pelt on the main wall, and a set of beaded curtains separated living room from kitchen. I hear he had plenty of wild parties there.

At that time, Richard was dating an Aboriginal girl who already had a child. "The Squaw," my father called her; he had rude names for everyone's dates. He had other choice names for her and Richard after she crashed his car, while under the influence of alcohol. Richard ended up with stitches on his face, and his car was totaled.

Beverly was moving out of the house too. She was tired of never having money, since my father took her pays for room-and-board. She always managed to find huge apartments for herself. I didn't like the changes. I missed having my brother and sister at home. But I found other ways to stay happy. Like the week Mom gave me permission to sleep in the tent Devon's father had set up for him in their backyard. Nearly ten-years-old, I'd never slept in a tent before. It looked to be pretty fun, and maybe just a bit scary. Little did I know, I was about to be re-introduced to cousin Mark's secret technique, and this time *I* would master the art of masturbation.

Our first night in the tent would prove to be a hit for all four of us: Devon, his brother Kenny, their cousin Jeremy, and myself. I can't recall if it was Devon's idea or his brother's, but one of them came up with a game we would all be winners at. We had two flashlights in the tent. I remember a deck of cards was used in the beginning, but would later be dropped. Somehow we used the cards to decide a loser. But this loser was still a kind of winner.

The flashlights would go off and the loser would have to chase the other three campers around the tent. Once he got a hold of someone, he had to properly identify his captive. If he named them incorrectly, he then had to jack that person off under the giggles and spotlights. As the game went on, it was obvious we could easily identify one another. So we changed the game rules as we went. No one wanted to catch Jeremy; that poor kid's penis was barely an inch—erect! He wasn't so much into playing the game as the three of us were. Who could blame him?

By the late hours of that first night, Devon and Kenny were checking out the ballooned lips on the head of my inflamed dick. (According to them, the state of my appendage meant something I should be proud of.) They seemed to know a lot about the penis. It's funny, not once did their parents come out to check on us. Not just that first night, but for the subsequent nights as well. We had no fear of being caught in the act. And on the third or fourth night in the tent, while the sun was still up, Jeremy's older sister paid us a visit. She must have been about fourteen-years-old, and none too shy about her own sexuality.

Kenny was probably about eleven-years-old himself. He convinced Stacey to flash us her tits if he were to flash her his dick. She agreed. So Kenny rose to his knees, dropped his drawers, and wiggled his flaccid penis in front of Stacey's face. We, of course, were all amused. She pretended not to be, but you could tell she was. And that's when Stacey raised her top and displayed her ample breasts to her little brother, her two cousins, and the boy from down the street.

As I recall, Jeremy didn't show up for the last couple nights of Camp Jack-Off. The brothers and I were eager to get back into our game. And since there was only the three of us now, we didn't have to pretend not to catch Jeremy. I would return home during the day to change clothes and freshen up. No one bothered me. And I was oblivious, yet, to the serious and eminent collapse of my home life.

My First Glimpse

Every morning I was awakened by our neighbor's blaring jukebox. He played "Raunchy" for the entire block. He should have kept it for his own ears. This guy had a large in-ground pool and deckhouse. He lived there with his wife and two kids, a son and daughter. A third son lived on his own just around the corner. If this neighbor's intrusive presence in my life hadn't inflicted the changes that it did , I would never bring him up.

The tent in Devon's backyard may have come down, but the game went on. I spent a lot of time playing with Devon and Kenny. I think Kenny even liked me, or, at least, I had something he liked. Devon and I started to change the way the game was played. We no longer needed the darkness, or to chase each other. We played in my room, his room, his basement, in my basement shower, and even in his shower while his family was eating breakfast right outside the door. No one questioned anything, except Richard, and only once. He asked me if Devon and I had taken a bath together. I lied and said no.

One night when Devon slept at my house we were too busy wrestling with the neighbor's son, who'd come to be my sister Tammy's boyfriend, to play any other type of game. The next day, Kenny was anxious to find out if we'd played the game. He seemed disappointed when we told him no. Then he went back to riding a wheelie all the way up the street on his bike—a trick he'd perfected.

Meanwhile, back at my house, having become friendly with our new neighbors, my father hired Mr.East to reface our washroom. (Dad was so naïve. He was never home.) And soon others were playing games of their own, with greater consequences. That washroom sure took a long time to get finished—all summer!

By then I'd hooked up with another little blond named Ashley.

She and Lynn were friends, and now Lynn had hooked up with Devon. It was a mismatch if ever there was one. Ashley and Devon were both blonds and she seemed taken by him, except he didn't measure up in the appearance department. And me, I still had a crush on Lynn, who had a crush on me. It didn't matter. Our pairing up didn't last much longer than a couple play days and a few forgettable pecks on the lips.

Guess I wasn't spending enough time at my own house because I failed to notice how much of her time my mother was spending with Mr. East. He was quite the show off, and I found his demeanor most unsettling. Mr. East loved to tell dirty jokes. Before long I knew them by heart because he repeated them to every new face that entered his backyard. Oh yeah, he was a connoisseur of comedy (about as much laughs as a funeral), a regular ladies man (Jabba the Hutt), a father to all children (the child catcher in *Chitty Chitty Bang Bang*)!

With Mom hanging out at Mr. East's house practically every day, drinking fancy mixers and enjoying her newfound habit of cigarette smoking, we kids (lured by pop cycles, Pepsi, and swimming) took to hanging out there a lot. I think public pools became extinct to us from that point on. Since Tammy was Tim's girlfriend, she was at the East's house steady. And that summer, I was briefly introduced to someone who would later become one of the most valued friends I'd ever know. Strictly speaking for myself, this friend is the only good thing I took away from meeting Mr. East. Dwayne was Mr. East's nephew from Delhi. He was shy at first and refused to come out to play. But once he did, it was like two long lost brothers had reunited. His stay was ending the night we finally got together. I was so disappointed when he went home. But in the very short hours we were getting to know each other, he'd left a permanent impression on me, and I on him.

The days began to drag a little. By mid summer, I was tiring of the game with Devon. He still wanted to play, but I was feeling apprehensive about it. I knew it was wrong. It had to be. Why else did we play in secrecy? Though I would say no to Devon more often than not, I still wanted to be touched, just not by him. Even playing the game with Kenny had lost its thrill. Kenny could lye back and let you jack him off for a freaking hour. See, we were still too young to reach a climax of any sort. Hell, we didn't even produce pre-come.

On one particular night at Devon's, after watching Kenny lift and drop his testicles without the use of his hands, he and Devon fell asleep. We'd made our beds on their bedroom floor, as we often did, and for some reason I was stricken with insomnia. But it was to my benefit that I'd been unable to join my friend's in slumber. Their house was so quiet and I was wide awake, staring out into their living room. And suddenly, there he was, Devon's father. He slowly crept passed the doorway, heading toward the washroom, and he was *naked*. I saw it all: his grown-up balls dangling below his grown-up cock, the thick line of hair that rose from his pubic area up to his navel, his left leg's hairy inner thigh. I listened to the sound of him relieving himself, waiting to see him cross my path again. As he sneaked through the darkness, I saw him turn and glance into our bedroom. I don't know if he saw my wide eyes. I felt that he did.

And you can bet your ass that the next day I was quick to share the news with Kenny and Devon. They were just as interested to hear me describe their father's penis as I was to describe it. And then they told me that when their mother had had some kind of operation, their dad had to masturbate for an extended period of time. Now, how they came to know this information, I can only guess. They knew many things about their parents that I didn't know, nor wanted to know, about my own.

Happy Birthday!

Summer did come to an end. I started grade five. Mr. East closed his pool for the winter. Dad continued to not be there. Devon's family moved away from our street. And I spent more time playing with Bi than with outsiders. We played *Wonder Woman* and *Bionic Woman* a lot—my two favorite shows. When I was bionic I wasn't Steve Austin, either, the man barely alive; I was Jamie Summers, fighting off Fembots. When Bi and I weren't play-fighting, we were really fighting. She'd scratch my arms and jab her fingernails into me, and I'd smack her back and make her cry—Good times.

With school in full swing, I resumed hanging out with Andy. During recess and lunch hours, he and I ran around the school building, hiding from Bird, who'd lost his nickname due to aging factors. He didn't seem to mind never actually catching up to us. And as we hid behind a dumpster one day, we raised ourselves up simultaneously to see if Ralf was coming. As if in slow-motion, the dumpster began to come down upon us. Andy slipped out from beneath it in time. I, however, was trapped like an idiot.

A recent addition to the school's faculty, Mr. Quickwhit, who'd seen the accident from the teacher's lounge room window, raced out to rescue me. I couldn't move. Miraculously, the only injury I sustained was a sprained big toe, and a crush to my pride. Mr. Quickwhit raised the dumpster off of me. He picked me up off the ground and ran back inside with me in his arms. Placing me gently on a chair, he examined my face and arms for injuries. My face must have been as red as a teacher's apple, I was so embarrassed.

I thought I was about to be screamed at or given detention. Turns out, they were just happy I wasn't seriously hurt. Mr. Quickwhit checked in on me later that afternoon, while I was in class. Come to think, all this commotion happened before the first morning bell. I remember because all my classmates were staring at me when we stood for the national anthem. Man, that toe hurt, throbbing in my shoe like Fred Flintstone's toe, after Barney dropped a bowling ball on it. That was my first encounter with Mr. Quickwhit, but it wouldn't be my last. Any drama that was happening to me personally at school, would soon take backseat to the events set in motion on the night of Mom's fortieth birthday party, orchestrated by none other than Mr. East. That single night easily distinguishes itself as my private introduction to hell.

Except for Richard, we were all present at Mr. East's house, including Dad. My mother's half sisters Jackie and Lorraine were there. And their sisters Pauline and Denise. Mom's cake was designed to look like an open book, which her sister had made, having recently taken a cake-decorating course. I think she baked it more to show herself off than as a gesture of her sisterly love. Things were running smoothly, till too much alcohol brought out the party girl in Mom. I'd never-EVER witnessed my mother drunk before. She was behaving in a giddy manner. My father wasn't saying much as he watched her. I think I would have felt the same way he did: it wasn't proper conduct in front of her young children. Especially when she squatted over a large ceramic pot my cousin had given her. First she pretended to pee, then she rubbed her crotch area with a little roll-on perfume. Nowadays her behavior would have been less a deal than it was then.

It was too much for Dad. He got up to leave. I don't understand why he didn't bother to take me by the hand to leave with him. But who knows what was going through his mind, or what he already knew had been going on. What I didn't witness, my sister Debbie did. She saw Mr. East grab my father by the throat and pin him up against the kitchen wall. He warned my father not to disrupt the party. Now I guess Dad went home for a few moments. He must have sat there contemplating what the hell had just happened, realized Mr. East was bullshit, and returned to collect us, and my mother. The party was over, but the war was just begun.

What I recall about the rest of that night: chaos at its best. My father on top of my mother in our kitchen stairwell. My mother trying to protect my father's head as Mr. East punched and clawed at him. When I saw that madman biting my father's ear, I kicked at his bald head, but I couldn't stop him (I vividly remember the wickedness in his dark eyes when he looked up at me). No one seemed able to control him. There was screaming between Mr. East's hefty daughter and my sisters outside. Mr. East's wife was in there, too, along with their daughter's goofy boyfriend. At one point, I watched Beverly and Debbie as they stood freaking out across the street. It was nothing short of insanity to me.

I don't know exactly how long the actual fighting went on; I'm sure the neighbor's would not soon forget. Since Mr. East's oldest son was now partnered up with Debbie, he tried to calm his father down and implement the peace, with little success. Much too late to protect anyone, the police arrived on the scene.

"Are you the one that called us?" one officer asked me.

I nodded yes.

"Do you see what you people are doing to this child?" he asked my parents.

I think I was then led up to bed. (My own fortieth birthday is coming up soon: I intend not to celebrate.)

That horrible night was the start of many nights of arguing between my parents. The arguing was constant. They argued during the nights, in the mornings, and at any time in which they were together in or around the house—Arguing. And by now, my mother's affair with Mr. East was no secret (Mom would often go out to bars with Mr. East and his wife. His wife even began to mimic Mom's attire to compete for her perverted husband's affections. I never understood what either woman saw in his ugliness—outwardly and inwardly.)

I couldn't concentrate at school; I was always wondering if my parents were arguing. I remember one night, when Mom and Dad had gone out, I had become so accustomed to their fighting that I couldn't sleep (I swore I could hear them). I literally had to get out of bed and peek into the living room from our stairway, just to be sure they weren't there.

One day I was pacing in front of Mr. East's house, avoiding the arguing that was blaring from my house, when a girl from my class happened by. She looked back at my house and said, "Oh, my God. Can you hear that?"

"I know," I answered.

"Do you live here?" she asked, directing her eyes at Mr. East's house.

"Yes," I said.

My life continued on in that way for quite some time. It wasn't until I came riding home with Debbie from her job one night, when Tim, who was sitting on his front porch steps, stopped us from going home.

"I wouldn't go there if I were you," he said.

Neither one of us had noticed him until the moment he spoke. We stopped our bicycles, exchanging looks of panic.

"Why? What's happened?" asked Debbie.

"Your Dad punched your Mom in the face. He's at the police station and your Mom's in my house."

And that was it. Those were the words we knew we'd hear eventually. I felt sick to my stomach. The quiet hours Debbie and I had just spent together at her variety store job were stripped away in an instant. Mom was inside, and her one eye was now a black and purple patch, with her eyeball under a bloody sleeve. It was far worse than I could have foreseen. We both ran in and hugged her, crying. Her embrace felt so weak, and I didn't feel strong enough to lift her up.

We got word that Dad was spending the night in jail, both to keep Mom safe, and keep him away from Mr. East. What I didn't know that night was that Mr. East had charged into our house when he and his family heard Mom's scream. I guess Dad had struck her outside, then dragged her into the house. Bi, who was six-years-old, got to watch her father straddle her mother and beat on her. She then witnessed the brawl between our deranged father and a self-serving Mr. East. She saw it all.

Dark Sunglasses, A Bible, And A Rocking Chair

WHAT I WOULDN'T HAVE given to return to the previous summer. My nerves, as well as my entire family's, were, as they say, shot to hell. Tammy, myself, and Bi were now staying at Mr. East's house with Mom. Debbie was staying with Joe, Mr. East's son. I heard and saw things while in Mr. East's house that even now I would not speak of. Let's just say I experienced countless moments of disappointment and disgrace in my parents when I was ten.

Richard had returned home with his fiancé to look after Dad. Tammy, Bi, and I had the great displeasure of having to visit our father. I wasn't alone in my loathing of that house, and the creature that sat waiting for us inside bore no resemblance to the dad we'd known. Two things in my life have scared the shit out of me: *The Exorcist*, and visiting Dad in our house after his meltdown.

Bi and I had to go in alone to see him. We stood side by side at the living room doorway. Dad had dimmed the wall sconces, leaving the room a murky yellow. He was slowly rocking in his chair, engulfed in cigarette smoke. Large dark Elvis glasses hid his eyes from us.

"Hi, guys," he drawled, his voice strained. "Come in and see me."

Bi and I looked to one another for reassurance before we walked over to him. He took this immense Catholic Bible off his lap and placed it on the table beside his chair (Dad with a bible was about as common a sight as tattoos on the Pope). Then he reached for Bi's hand and directed her to sit on his lap. She was terrified, I could tell. We both wanted to bolt out of there. He took his glasses off, saying, "See what they did to me."

Dad's eye looked like he'd been kicked by a horse. It was far worse than Mom's. It was disgusting, and we couldn't believe he was showing it to us. He was acting so weird, so...Norman Bates. We didn't want to go back there. He was too incoherent—too fucking creepy!

I Wanna Go Home

It wasn't long before Mom moved us out of Mr. East's and into an old war-time house just down the street. Three little bedrooms, washroom, kitchen, and living room. It was a hole compared to our grandparents' house. It was a hole compared to a hole. Mr. East continued to take Mom out. Bi and I were alone a lot. We hadn't changed our opinions about Dad either: he was still weird. He'd come around our school looking for us, driving his old pickup. I hated that truck, especially the hand-sized crucifix he'd hung from the rearview-mirror.

"Isn't that your dad?" kids would say.

"Nope," I'd answer, hiding myself from his sight.

As time went by, Dad's drive-bys decreased. He got rid of the glasses and stopped trying to preach the gospel to Bi and I. As we fell under another Ontario winter, we began to see signs of the normal man again. And on Sundays, Dad had permission to have visits with his two youngest. We usually went for burgers at a cheap restaurant or something, but for this coming weekend, he told us to dress extra warm because we were going ski-doing.

We drove out to a beach-house, where Dad's long-time friend, Pat, lived. We'd all known Pat forever. He and his partner, Scott, had been friends with my parents for many years. They'd even traveled together on several vacations to the likes of Mexico and Washington. I personally hadn't seen him for a few years. Since we had time to kill, waiting for our Uncle Pete to arrive with his kids, Bi and I ran down to the snowy beach. I was already wondering why our day was taking so long to begin. I hadn't noticed any snow-mobiles, either, and that was because there weren't any.

Dad called for us to come back up the hill, where he led us into Pat's camper. He opened these large drawers to show us the abundance of goodies in store: licorice, cookies, chips, and chocolate bars. I was already sensing a change of plans at work. Uncle Pete's daughter showed up with her younger sister at her side; Kendra was about to play mommy for the next three weeks. She climbed aboard with Jenny as Dad sat behind the wheel to take us out, with Eddie Rabbit's "I Love A Rainy Night," playing on the radio.

I didn't get it. What happened to our ski-do ride? And no one told us Uncle Pete and his kids were coming. We stopped in the parking lot of a grocery store to wait for Billy—Uncle Pete's son. Billy was a year or two younger than I, and he was late. Uncle Pete and Dad seemed anxious about his tardiness. Pete blasted him when he finally came running up to the camper. As Billy made excuses for being late, Dad drove us beyond the city limits, and that's when I began to question him about this plan.

"Where are we going? You know we have to be home by dark, and it's already getting there," I said.

Dad tried to keep me calm, with Pete and Kendra's help. They told me we were going to some place called miniature land, where everything was small. But I knew they were lying. I insisted on knowing the truth; and so, after realizing I wasn't going to give up, they told me. We were off to Florida (British Columbia). We had relatives there to visit. We were going to buy a whole new wardrobe. Dad even promised me a pair of new cowboy boots, which I wanted because he always wore them.

"You can't do this. This is kidnapping!" I said, furious that I'd been deceived.

"You can't kidnap your own kids," Dad replied, with Kendra and Uncle Pete agreeing.

"Ah, Yes, you can, and this is it," I persisted.

But my opinion didn't matter. I was surrounded by idiots who were now in control of my life. I remained silent, angry, and in disbelief for the rest of that first night. It would be days before Dad stopped to phone Mom, with his demands that she come back to him or she would never see her two children again (you know, since we were in Florida). Uncle Pete wasn't just along for the ride, he was playing out the same stupid plan as Dad. He phoned his wife and made the same ridiculous demands, with her three children as the ransom.

Our drive out to B.C. took us seven days. By the fourth night, and after nonstop complaining from all of us kids, Dad and Pete finally pulled into a motel for us to get showered. I remember this place well. There was a couple diesel trucks parked in the middle of the stony road, idling. But I didn't see a single soul around. There was just this one little street, the dingy motel, and us. We discovered that you had to put coins in the bloody shower. I'm not sure why Dad and Pete were in such a rush, but Billy and I weren't even given a chance to shower (I would have to wait another three days).

While we were stopped to fuel up at a gas-station, Bi and I were plotting our grand escape. The camper was so dirty on the outside, I was able to write a clear message on the rear window, without Dad and Pete noticing. As soon as we hit the highway, Bi and I were on our knees at the back of the camper, waving to the cars driving behind us, trying to get their attention. But, alas, it would seem that Canadians in the eighties didn't take a giant finger-written message on the window of a filthy camper, with two children waving hysterically, too seriously.

HELP US! WE'VE BEEN KIDNAPPED!

I'm not sure how far we'd traveled before Dad and Pete found us out, and were outraged. They wiped the window clean and screamed at me, but they knew I didn't care. Dad started to make more frequent calls home to Mom. He didn't allow us to hear the first couple conversations, nor were we allowed to speak to her. It wasn't until we were in the mountains at a place called Crow's Nest that he allowed us to say hello. But he wasn't quick enough to grab the phone away from Bi, before she revealed the secret of our location. She couldn't help it, there was a giant sign of a nest with a crow in it just above our heads. And that was the clue to help Mom discover our whereabouts. Still, no leads for Mom and her lawyer would do us any good. We'd never be rescued like in the movies. We would just have to ride out this horrible adventure.

Dad left us in our grungy clothes. He purchased a T-shirt and a pair of socks for me during the second week. I wasn't impressed with anything. Bi and I were prisoners. We were told we'd be starting school there, but Dad learned quickly what a stubborn son I could be. I threatened to expose him the first chance I got. He must have heard me tell him I hated his guts at least thirty times a day. My young mind could not understand why no one else thought our kidnapping was wrong. Our so-called relatives were all morons—every last one of them!

Trapped in the mountains of a place called Salmoe, in what seemed like the deepest recess in the world, under a heavy snowfall, I wandered out to visit the horse I'd seen gated up in a thick of pine trees. I pat his fuzzy nose as he fed on straw. He didn't pay me no mind. I was so sad. I began to sing that old Bobby Bare song about going home.

"I wanna go home. I wanna go home. Oh, how I wanna go home. Last night I went to sleep in Detroit city. I dreamed about my Momma, dear ole Pappa, sister and brother. I dreamed about the…"

I turned with a start, caught in my moment of serenity by my father. I don't remember what he said, but I always wondered just how long he'd been standing there, listening. And something happened between Bi and I during those weeks, something I believe probably only occurs when people are older than we were: we connected. We set a bond in place that may have only come years later, or maybe never. But it came to us when we were standing atop a snowy hill, with a plastic carpet we'd taken from beside one of the A-Frame houses. Between runs down the hill on the carpet, we noticed a small rainbow drifting between us in a cloud of mist. We were entranced by it, this colorful hint of hope.

Dad left us alone a lot; guess he knew there was no place for us to run to. One day we drove to another dinky town, where he left us to wait in the camper. I think we were at the house of the guy who would later take us to pan for gold. Yeah, you read that correctly: Panning For Gold! While Dad was inside, Bi and I stepped out of the camper, pulled our elbows through the ends of our sweater sleeves, with our hands on our shoulders, and tried to stop traffic in the guise of amputees. Yeah, you read *that* right, too! Needless to say, we didn't accomplish much, but it was good for a laugh—later.

I think another week past before we finally packed ourselves up, Uncle Pete and his clan as well, and headed for home. I couldn't believe they'd come to their senses. Meanwhile, Mom and her lawyer were a day behind in their rescue attempt. It didn't matter, we were heading home, and three days later, we *were* home. Bi and I both recall how we were walking from Dad's house back to Mom's down the street, afraid to look back, for fear that Dad might have changed his mind in freeing us. We held hands and started to run as fast as we could. Upon opening the front door at Mom's house, she turned to face us with the telephone receiver held to her ear.

"Yes. They're here," she said, weeping.

She hung the phone up and opened her arms to us (and that was our mother).

I'm brought to tears even now by the memory of it. It took years for me to find it in my heart to forgive my father. He'd stripped us of our trust in him. He'd starved us, feeding us nothing more than junk foods. He'd left us for days without being able to bathe. He'd forced us into the company of strangers. He'd made me wash dishes in the snow—that bastard. And worst of all: he'd kept us from our mother and siblings.

On a sillier note, Bi and I never forgot how our sister, Tammy, had told us she loved us at the end of one of our telephone calls home. Tammy?...Love?...Us? We couldn't stop discussing what it meant. This really is serious, if *Tammy* can say she loves us!

Needless to say, it took a while before Bi and I would dare return to Dad's. I believe Mom celebrated our return by bringing us to the old Park Theater to see Lilly Tomlin in *The Incredible Shrinking Woman*. It was perfect. Mom knew just how to warm our hearts again. And back at school, well, that was a different story. I couldn't understand how the hell everyone knew I'd been kidnapped. Then I found out that Debbie, during a moment of desperation, wrote on the school window, "Please pray for Michael and

BiBianne, they've been kidnapped!"

Yeah, that's our Debbie.

My Own Mr. Kotter

During the next summer, between grade five and six, Dwayne returned to Welland. Only this time he would stay at our house and not at his uncle's. He and I had something special between us, something that could only be described as spiritual. We were from such diverse backgrounds, and yet, no two souls could ever be more implicitly entwined.

Sure, we did stupid little boy things while growing up. Sex and our sexual parts are a major influence in life. So, like any two normal young lads who often found themselves changing together to go swimming, we'd make our penis lips talk, or make their heads touch (oh, come on, we've all done it. Those of us *with* penises). We did our share of skinny-dipping and wiggling our penises under water too. (It's okay to chuckle.)

Sure, we jacked off together. Big deal. With Dwayne and Me, nothing we ever did was lustful. I may have touched his, he may have touched mine, but you know what I'm saying. We weren't sexually attracted to one another, we were just being human (and perhaps a little horny). When you're together night and day, nudity just becomes an extension of how you relate to one another. And with each passing summer, our friendship would set itself amongst the stars, unattainable by anything or anyone to meddle with.

Without fail, I always needed a week or so to get over the sadness I felt when Dwayne would leave. Grade six had begun, and would prove to be the best elementary school year I'd ever experience. And it was all thanks to my old rescuer, Mr. Quickwhit. I couldn't have been more pleased to discover he was my teacher. This guy was hilarious. We rarely got any work done in his class. He seemed content to get to know each one of us as individuals, and through comic relief.

He never checked our homework or our in-class work. This made it so easy for myself and a couple female students to cheat for each other when we were correcting our work. If you had a certain amount of errors, you'd have to redo the assignment. So, of course, we were sure to nix those 'too many' errors. But more important than our cheating skills was Mr. Quickwhit himself. His hair was light brown, naturally curly, and pretty much looked like an Afro. He wore a thick mustache that matched his hair color, and dark-framed glasses. Not only did he behave like, but he looked like Gabe Kaplan on *Welcome Back Kotter*.

We had a great year with Mr. Quickwhit. It seemed that every other teacher was jealous of his popularity with our class. We weren't an easy class to teach. We had more than our share of troublemakers. But for Mr. Quickwhit, no one was trouble. He was too much fun for the rotten kids to upset. Besides, I don't think he could be upset. By mid year, he'd made us a deal: If everyone behaved from that point until the end of the year, he'd throw us a party at his parent's beach-house.

There were times when we thought that party would never happen, but it did. And at the end of the school year, Mr. Quickwhit invited our class to the beach. A few volunteer parents supplied our ride there. None of us were thrilled when the school principal dropped by. She was a nun. A rather miserable nun (is there any other kind?) She brought some goodies, said hello, probably just wanted to snoop, then left.

I remember playing ball on the beach, swimming, munching. I remember having to change out of our wet bathing suits in the garage with the other boys in my class. That was the very first time we had to reveal our nakedness to each other. Now, I don't know if girls ever pray for big boobs, but I prayed for hairy legs when I was younger, and my prayers were answered. I had hairy legs, a mustache (which the other kids made fun of) and I had pubic hair. I wasn't aware that puberty hadn't visited my classmates yet.

Ralf was changing a few feet next to me. He was shocked to see me drop my suit so nonchalantly. "Aren't you embarrassed?" he whispered to me.

"No," I said, shrugging my shoulders.

Then I noticed one of my classmates checking me out. He was one of the more mature students. So, I checked him out, and didn't see much. It was then that I realized he wasn't the only one checking me out. And as I glanced about from those gazing eyes to those tiny hairless parts, the embarrassment kicked in. I quickly pulled my shorts up, grabbed my wet suit, and rushed out of there.

Supper was hotdogs and hamburgers, with potato chips and soda. And afterward, we all enjoyed a bonfire on the beach. It was dark by the time we started packing up. Ralf, Andy, and myself were suddenly the only three left. All the other students and parents had gone. Mr. Quickwhit was going to give us a ride home. How we got so lucky, I don't know. I don't think I ever caught a glimpse of Mr. Quickwhit's parents, but I know they were home because I heard him talking to someone in the house.

Ralf and Andy were tossing a ball to one another as I sat on the concrete steps of the front porch. I heard Mr. Quickwhit's voice again, so I turned, and there he was, standing in the doorway, changing out of his day clothes into night clothes. He didn't see me watching him. He had reddish hair on his chest and legs. I didn't see him completely naked; he didn't change his briefs, or had already. But I saw more than any other student in my class had seen of him. The thing is, I didn't feel aroused by it; I felt like I was somehow closer to the person than the teacher. I told Andy I'd seen Mr. Quickwhit changing. He just said, "So."

The ride home was fun. Andy and I were rolling around in the back of Mr. Quickwhit's empty van, while Ralf, of course, sat in the passenger's seat, babbling on. I was the first to be dropped off. I think Mr. Quickwhit was amused with me. I could tell by the things he'd say. I think he was surprised to see me let loose, being the quiet kid in class that I was.

It was unfortunate that he didn't stick around. He'd dropped in like a *Mary_Poppins*, treated us to the best year we'd have in public school, then disappeared. It wasn't until grade eight that he paid us a surprise visit. He stopped in to say hello to our class for a moment one day. And of all people, he fingered *me* out. He asked me to stand up so he could see how tall I'd grown. Said he couldn't believe I was little Michael. Plus, don't forget, I was the stupid kid he'd rescued from under the dumpster.

I felt so shy. When I sat down, I wondered if he'd pick out anyone else, like the students he'd laughed with so much in grade six—the more popular faces. But he didn't. That was it. I was it. His smiling face left our room and I never saw him again. Never forgot him either.

Enter At Your Own Risk

In answer to my mother's prayers, and countless applications, we were accepted into a Housing contract for low income families. Leaving Wallace behind, we moved into a large duplex in a clean neighborhood on—appropriately named—Victory Avenue. Life was pretty good there—quiet. I graduated from St. Andrew's in what was as lame a ceremony as I'd ever seen: in the basement of the Church, of course. And following another summer with Dwayne, I followed my sister Tammy into high school.

Westbrook Secondary School was the choice I'd made. It was the only high school that offered a slue of shop classes in its curriculum. But Mom had to argue with the bigwigs to get me in. See, not only was Westbrook unique because of the shops, it was also designed for slower learners and kids who had trouble performing at top levels. I thought I fit the bill perfectly, but some officials didn't think so. I knew that if I went to any of the other city high schools I would struggle with my grades. After three meetings, Mom had won on my behalf.

As I was entering my first year, Tammy was entering her last. She was beautiful; honestly, the best-looking chic there. I saw high school as an opportunity to finally break free from the dull student I'd been and become someone new and exciting, someone other kids would want to hang with. And that's exactly what I did, for the first month or so. I was so ecstatic to begin anew that I didn't have to try to be likeable, I just was. Unfortunately, I was attracting the riff-raff. I was being invited to all the parties, which I'd never attend (I wasn't the partying type). And the instant the thrill of high school wore off and reality set back in, all the riffs and all the raffs saw me for what I truly was—humdrum.

A few kids I'd initially met at the start drifted away from me as well; or rather, I drifted quietly away from them. There were a couple nice kids, but too immature for me. Andy had joined me at the same high school, but that long time friendship waned. He started to use the workout room a lot, and became part of a clique of guys whose only focus was on how much weight they could bench press, and how hard their pectorals were.

Settling in at Westbrook was easy. The one thing I hadn't prepared myself for, however, was the new array of bullies I was soon to deal with. How many fucking times must a man endure such bullshit? Well, let me tell you—it never goes away. Maybe the faces of the bullies change, maybe they're not even all male, but under that exterior hides the bully, the thorn in your side, the prick in your thumb, the pain in your ASS!

I encountered bullies aplenty. I'll leave them all nameless because these people do not deserve their names in print, unless it's naming them in an arrest in your local paper. There was the tall kid, who I'd eventually bribe in grade twelve, with a peace offering in the form of a cheap gold necklace, his favorite rock band's logo dangling on the end. Yes, four years of that A-hole. There was the chunky Negro who came to our school late in the year. I was his object to poke fun at on a daily basis. And there was even a little guy. I don't think he stood taller than your typical seven-year-old. Didn't stop him from picking on me. I wonder: what was it about me that drew them to harass me? Was *Lisa Simpson's* bully theory right?

Anyway, that's all I have to say about the bullies. Two chapters dedicated to them are more than enough. Besides, they were there to make life interesting, right? The good kids I met certainly outnumbered the bad. Kids like my friends Tom and Darren, Andre, Wayne, Huey, Denise, Doris, Lenny, and so many more. And I encountered a couple surprises such as Carla and Judy! Yeah, my old flames were there, too, still girl pals at that.

There are a couple reasons why grade nine was a shitty year for me. The first is shit itself. Not that it was the start of my disease, but it had never interfered with my schooling before. Irritable Bowel Syndrome (IBS) was pulling me out of my classes every day. To roam the halls, students had to carry a wooden key with them from each classroom. Well, I would take the key and disappear to the washroom to suffer through my cramps and diarrhea, and wouldn't return to that class until a couple hours later. You could tell I was a good student because not one of the teachers ever questioned me about it.

The second reason my year sucked was because I was stuck in a nightmare of stereotypical male shops. And then I met Doug. Ours was an unusual pairing. He was awesome in shop classes like Auto body, Small Engines, Building Construction, and Metal Fab. All of which he carried me through. I liked him so much. He was my new best friend. He and I had some great times, messing around in class. Even Doug, whom I saw as a tough character, fell victim to 'the tall kid's' bullying at times. I don't know what I would have done without Doug that year.

Not two months later, Tammy and I switched buses. The Lincoln Street bus had fewer students on it and half the ruckus. It was on that bus I met a pair of sisters named Elly and Mona. Though they were in my grade, I hadn't noticed them before. Elly was a brunette, and a little taller than her blond sister. I didn't take an immediate interest in them. Mona drew attention to herself with the bright red lipstick she wore. I took to teasing her about it, calling her Red or Lips. Don't get the wrong idea here: my teasing of Mona wasn't one of those 'boy teases girl 'cause he likes her' deals. Those damned lips made her an easy target. (Oh my God!—*I* was Mona's *bully*!)

When grade nine ended, and thank goodness it did, Doug and I kept in contact with each other on the phone. He didn't live in Welland. This prevented us from ever getting together outside of school. Summer was fine. Dwayne lived at our house as usual. He and I rode our bikes to Niagara Falls quite often. We had our photos taken in those little booths, bought rock n' roll pins, and enjoyed ourselves. We still jacked off together once in a while, when there was nothing else to do. And then, just like always, Dwayne was gone. I never got used to his leaving. It always hurt.

Grade ten was on the horizon. Doug and I were spending hours talking to each other on the phone. We were catching up on what we'd missed through the holidays, planning what we might do at school—tomorrow! When I got off the bus the next day, I searched the familiar faces of the last year. Noticed the new faces of the fresh kids; they seemed to get shorter every year. But Doug's smiling face was nowhere to be seen. I waited and watched as the last buses arrived, and still, no Doug. I couldn't understand what had happened. I'd just spoken with him the night before. Where was he?

That entire day dragged for me. I couldn't wait to get back home and call my friend; we connected on my first try. Doug then told me he'd moved during the summer and had to change schools—I was stunned. Was he afraid to tell me the night before? I don't recall what his reason was for leaving me in the dark, but he'd played one hell of a cruel joke on me. The following day at school, I frowned my way from class to class. I kept thinking that at any moment Doug was going to walk in, but he never did.

Despite the loss of my good friend, grade ten looked to be more enjoyable than its predecessor. Having already been forced to sample a mixture of shops, year two students were allowed to choose their classes. Finally, I no longer had to venture into that section of the school, where the grease monkey's played with their engines. I'd learned the difference between cement and concrete. I'd mixed, jig-sawed, soldered, sanded, painted, and screwed; and now I was free to choose. I chose: Typing, Business Machines, Art, Horticulture, Restaurant Services, Chef Training, and Hospital Services.
I was the only male in the Typing and Business Machines classes. We learned how to type on Manual typewriters. I was a fast learner, and I made a lot of girl friends. Elly and Mona were in those classes. They were in many of my classes. We became a threesome, even being mocked by some students who labeled us Jack, Janet, and Chrissy (the trio from the 80's sitcom *Three's Company*). Some guys made fun of me, while others envied me.

Very rarely was I apart from Janet and Chrissy—I mean—Elly and Mona. Our own little group soon formed, consisting of Sean, Jim, Nancy, Lori, Darren and Laury, and Julie—but not really Julie, she just invited herself in. Julie had known Elly and Mona from public school, and they couldn't seem to shake her. The thing about high school: friendships are settled into. You have to meet a lot of people before you can meet your true friends.

Early into our friendship, I'd let Elly know my feelings were strong toward her. She gave me that, 'I think of you as the brother I never had' bit. Yeah, that's what a guy with four sisters at home wants to hear from the girl he's sweet on. But rather than force the issue and endanger the friendship, as it was, I chose to back down. It was better to hang with Elly as her chum than not at all. Besides, I wasn't about to give up that easily.

My friendship with Sean was slow in developing. He was someone I could call on after school to hang with. He was a good guy, just not a hundred percent my type. At least he wasn't hyper (there, I said something nice about him). Admittedly, I did check out his not-so-hairy legs when we were tanning once or twice. I could have checked out his junk up close one time, but I didn't. He'd taken me to swim at the local university. And after our swim, standing right next to me in the showers, he reached up and hung his swimsuit on the towel-line. Shocked, I told him I was going into the sauna for a few minutes, and rushed out of there. Yeah, I'd avoided seeing Sean's junk, only to sit in a steamy room with ten other men and their dangling treasures. (Poor Me—there was no escaping!)

That same year I entered myself into a modeling gig for a local clothing store. It was the first of four shows I would do for them. But instead of a strut down a runway the models had to dance. I was a good dancer. Copying moves I'd seen on MTV came naturally to me. I made a few fans with that first show, and even got hired to work at the store. But the manager, this wig-wearing bitch, fired me when I turned down an offer to cover someone else's shift. I didn't care. The weight of thirty pairs of jeans on my left arm, while I spread the jeans on the rack to make room for the new ones, nearly broke my back. And besides, what fifteen-year-old wants to spend his summer working?

Testosterone

Dwayne was back. I introduced him to my new friends. Elly and Mona seemed to like him. Mona didn't hang with us much, but Elly did. I recall feeling something one time that was new to me: jealousy. The three of us had been swimming in Mr. East's pool, but I was the first to come out. I wasn't aware of it, but my heart was tuckering me out. I had to rest. And as I sat shivering with a towel wrapped around myself, I watched Dwayne and Elly at play. The frolicking between them was innocent, of course. I wanted them to be friends. I wanted them to like one another, didn't I? I never told Dwayne how uncomfortable I was with his and Elly's bonding: that would have been frivolous.

Why'd I Wear That Vest?

Halfway. Two years down, and two to go. Grade eleven would be the defining year for me. My friendship with Elly and Mona was solidified. Even had I not had any male friends on the side, the bond I had with the sisters would have sufficed. By now, teachers had come to know who's who of the student body. My wonderful Art instructor, whom we called Mr. F., took a special interest in our threesome. Although our last names were different, he somehow thought we were brother and sisters. Whatever.

Every chance Mr. F. got, he'd sign a note excusing the three of us from other classes to work on Art projects. These projects were supposed to be different signs and shit for special school events (we had an awful lot of events). Any time I'd hand a teacher one of Mr. F.'s notes, they'd roll their eyes and repeat his name like he was some evil villain up to no good...again. "Furguson." They knew we were getting a free ticket to do nothing, while listening to Pink Floyd's *The Wall* and Prince's *Purple Rain* (Mr.F.'s two favorite albums). It was awesome. For myself, it meant more time with Elly that no one else could interfere with.

It was about that time that this guy in grade twelve began to ask me a lot of questions about Elly. He rode my bus home and actually lived on my street. There was no eluding him, or his infatuation with the object of my affections. And more to my dismay, Elly had shown an interest in *him*! Ironically, I was in a position to make or break this affair, so I broke it. I told him she wasn't interested, and I told her what a moron he was. Poor fellow, he didn't stand a chance with me in the picture. So I'd averted that mess, but there would be another.

In the early fall, chosen unanimously by the staff, five grade eleven students would be sent to Leadership Camp to represent the school. Five or more promising students from every other local high school in the Niagara area would also attend. Not so much to our surprise, being the well-behaved, level-headed, hard-working students that we were; Elly, Mona, Julie, Jim, and myself were the chosen. The three day, two night stay at Leadership Camp came at no cost to any of us.

The bus ride to camp with a load of strangers was a bit unsettling, and exciting. One passenger—this big idiotic loser—made his presence known immediately. And lucky Jim and I would have to put up with the goof's shenanigans in our cabin as well. It was obvious to me that his school chose to send him in order to get rid of him for three days, and not for his great personality.

One night in our cabin, he pulled out a leather bondage whip and threatened some of the boys with it, including Jim, who was too naïve to recognize insults when they were being thrown at him. I, on the other hand, gave him a stern stare, turned my back on the creep and his entourage, and he didn't bother me. And now that I think about it, I'll bet our starving-for-attention, whip wielding hero was gay! Seems to me he enjoyed physically teasing the boys a bit too much.

Although the camp curriculum dealt us some hokey lessons about cold pricklies and warm fuzzies, and bore moments reminiscent of scenes from the television movie *Guyana Tragedy: The Story of Jim Jones*, all in all I had fun. I met some good kids. For our last night there we were separated into groups. Each group was to come up with a play or any type of entertainment to share in front of the entire camp. Jim, again too naïve to realize his weaknesses, put himself on the list as a break dancer. Remember break dancing? I had a few moves myself, but to get up in front of everyone and perform for the length of Herbie Hancock's "Rockit?" Never! But Jim did.

I wasn't the only one feeling sorry for him as he ran out of steam. An oriental girl who was sitting next to me said, " Why don't you go out there and save him?"

"No thanks," I replied. "One fool is enough."

She laughed. "You're right! I'm Amy," she introduced. She

was tiny and cute and talkative. We sat together through the entire show.

When it was my group's turn to perform, I didn't leave my seat. Under the guidance of a prissy girl, they'd come up with an act about Michael Jackson and Mr. T. Since I was the only student at camp who showed up wearing a black version of M.J.'s "Beat It" video jacket, they borrowed it, in vest form, for their act. They didn't need me, they had my vest. I felt that they were insulting me, personally, but I let it go as if I was undaunted. Their act went off without the laughs they were sure they'd elicit.

Then it was my turn. And what lame-ass routine did I come up with on my own? Two girls put makeup on my face and lent me a girly top to wear. I walked out into the center of everyone's attention and began to jump up and down. I did this for about a minute, leaving them wondering what the fuck I was supposed to be doing. And then I said loud and clear, "Don't look at me. Look at my hair. It's bouncing and behaving." Then I stopped jumping and walked off the stage to silence. Was I the only one that got the joke? I don't know. I didn't ask anyone afterward. If I'd been on *The Gong Show*, I'm sure the gong would have saved me before the punch-line.

The next morning, we gathered in the main hall for a stupid song and breakfast. Before breakfast, I'd gone into the washroom, and that's where I met David. He was about two feet taller than I, with thick blond hair and blue eyes. I don't know how I hadn't noticed this delicious giant before now. I was quite disappointed that I'd met him at the end of camp and not at the start. Some of the other boys had toilet-papered the ceiling. David and I agreed it was childish. We were instant friends. He and I walked back into the main hall together.

"Do you want to sit at my table?" he asked.

"Sure," I said.

I followed him to his table, where he was about to introduce me to his good friend and school chum, *Amy*!

"Yeah!" Amy exclaimed. "We met last night. Sure. Mike is such a good guy."

So, there I was, sitting in between Amy and David and wishing it was my permanent place in life. And they weren't boyfriend and girlfriend, either. When I think back to the way David looked at me, I think David and I had much more in common than we would ever share. I remember smiling across the room at Elly and Mona, who were probably wondering what I was doing at another table.

Shortly after breakfast, speeches were given by the counselors, goodbyes were passed around, and we began to board the buses. David and Amy were giving me hugs and promises to call and write. Amy and I even exchanged earrings; I still have hers. That wasn't our last goodbye. Elly, Mona, Jim, and I would soon attend a high school dance in Sherkston, where we'd been invited by David and Amy. I later exchanged a few letters with Amy, always asking about David. But the letters would eventually stop, and David and Amy would fade into the past.

Pink Says...What?

Following on the heels of our camp experience, Elly, Mona, and I were being chosen for other school activities. We ran the chocolate bar campaign, for whatever they were trying to raise money for. That got us out of more class time. Then we were off to do a blitz fundraiser for the United Way. More time away from classes. One teacher who seemed to be involved with all the extracurricular goings on was Mr. Mitler. He was a short man, with very blue eyes and dark curly hair. I used to daydream about possible private encounters he and I could have. Maybe in the back of his car or, I don't know, different scenarios. My crush on him didn't rule my life or anything. We only had him for one class. But he was good to talk to. He didn't treat us like kids. And usually our opinion about another teacher was either enlightened or agreed upon by him.

I remember some kind of trip came up that I couldn't go on, for lack of money or something, and Mr. Mitler was going on that trip. I was pretty downhearted about not going and missing my chance to (maybe if I got lucky) brush up against him (accidentally of course). An intimate moment shared with the man would never happen. Mitler knew I had a thing for Elly, and he also knew she wasn't responding. He never gave me advice in that area or anything, but during one of our school's video dances, he gave me a wink and a nod as I was dancing with Elly. I think he was dancing with Mona.

Away from school, I participated in two more fashion shows. For the first show I had to do a lot of Michael Jackson video routines—it was fun, but not really the type of dancing I was capable of, and enjoyed. I made the local newspaper for that show. I was surprised that no one at school teased me about the modeling. By the third fashion show, we were booked to perform at a local hotel. I was practicing daily for this particular event. Since I had become the most popular dancer in the shows, and I say this humbly, I was finally given the chance to perform alone. I was determined to prove there was more to my dancing skills than mimicking Jackson.

So when I got up on that stripper platform with those lights coruscating, the intro to Prince's "Let's Go Crazy" blaring, my heart bruising my chest walls, and all those eyes focused on me; I let them have it. Initially, I was only supposed to dance for half of the song, but once I got going, I lost all sense of time, and no one stopped me. Tammy was also in that show; I'd convinced her to join us. She later told me that several people dragged her out of the change room to come and watch my performance, yelling excitedly, "It's your brother! He's dancing!"

My brother Richard was also at that performance. He was in the audience with his wife and my mother. He never said a word to me about the show. So I never knew what he thought. It was my big moment of fame. Again I made the local paper, looking not at all like myself in the photo. That show, as cheesy as it was, gave quite a boost to my self-confidence. Too bad it would only last until the fourth and final show, which came later that same year, just in time for the fall and winter clothing line.

Had I known what a flop the last show was going to be, I would have kept myself out of it. The wig-wearing bitch decided to book us into a small hall with an RSVP audience only. Guess she thought she was some kind of Big-Wig-Fashion Show-Mogul. A few people bought tickets knowing that I was going to be in the show again. What they didn't know, nor I, was that there wasn't going to be any dancing. The one aspect of the shows that made them at all interesting and fun, Ms. Big-Wig decided to take out.

A new addition to our modeling crew was this tiny man who was out in a big way. He styled his hair in that typical new wave flip, wore a blond beard and mustache in an attempt to look more mature, and was soft-spoken. I thought he was attractive but something about him made me a homophobe. While we were changing from outfit to outfit, he revealed his pink socks, which matched his pink bikini briefs. They weren't simply pink either. They were that type of fluorescent pink that was so popular during the Frankie Goes To Hollywood *80's*.

Another man in the show was also queer, but he was a more subdued queer. Nothing about him screamed Queer. Perhaps that's what triggered my negative feelings toward Mr. Pink Undies: the cute little guy was screaming. The funny thing about it all is that I never caught them checking me out as we changed. I mean, sure, I was just a punk, but you never know. Meanwhile, there I was checking *them* out, and making judgments.

Exit At Your Own Risk

Year four—grade twelve. Still a threesome, (and out of sheer boredom) Elly, Mona, and I started to frequent a local bar that neglected to check IDs. Actually, Elly and I were just following Mona. She'd already been hanging out at this bar, and had already dated several guys—mostly yuppies. At least in those days she dolled herself up to go out (probably to put on an older appearance). We were introduced to her little gang of friends. As I remember it, I think we did a lot of sitting in booths, smiling, and sipping one drink for a couple hours.

When the bar got busy on weekends we'd get up and dance. Sip…and dance. And remember that bully I played ring-around-the-mailbox with? Well, I came face to face with him one night in that bar. Okay, it was more like his face at my chest level. That's right, he hadn't grown very tall. It was one of those rare moments in life when you get to have the last smug, self-satisfying grin, as it were. No words were exchanged. He recognized me and I recognized him. He was short and I was tall—taller—tall enough that it made all the difference. And it felt fucking great!

I also met the 'next someone' in that bar—Elly's next someone. Her choosing this guy as her boyfriend would come as quite a shock to me and Mona. Though Elly would, in later years, deny the memory of our first meeting with Dan, my memory would not forget it. We were sitting at a round table when he came to join us. Mona'd already met and disliked him. And as Elly and I sat on one side of the table, Dan sat next to Mona, opposite us.

From where I was sitting, I could see him putting his hand on Mona's lap. She kept swiping it away in disgust. I couldn't stand him. He was so full of himself and such a jerk. At least three times he tried the hand on Mona's lap. When he finally walked away,

Elly expressed her disliking of him. At that moment I thought we all agreed that Dan was a loser.

About two weeks later, Elly invited Mona and I to meet her at the bar so she could introduce the new love of her life to us. I couldn't believe it. Who was this new boyfriend and when the hell did she have time to get to know this mystery man. *I* was usually with her. Well, the big night came around and off we went to unveil Elly's secret affair. I don't need to tell you how discombobulated I was at the sight of Dan and Elly holding hands. I thought, *What the fuck? Isn't this the same asshole we all agreed was an asshole? Isn't this the asshole who was putting the moves on her sister?*

Elly acted all skittish, just a ball of little girl with her fantastic new boyfriend. And I stood there dumbfounded and heartbroken and thought, *What the Fuck*? First chance I got to be alone with Mona, I ran my confusion past her, asking, "Wasn't he the asshole making passes at you?"

Mona was no less stunned than I was. And what neither of us could figure out was—WHEN? When did this big love affair begin—and HOW? And WHY? We'd soon have our answers. You see, Elly and Mona helped put a good word in for me at the Bakery, where they continued to work with their mother. I was soon hired to work with them. It wasn't a great job but it was easy. And working with Elly and Mona made it fun. So, at seventeen, I began my first real job.

But I wasn't the only new employee. Someone else had been hired not long before me, as a driver—Dan. His job was to deliver the bakery's products to local grocery stores and such. Thank heaven he wasn't working with us, or even with the bakers. I don't think I could have handled his presence on a regular basis. I don't recall even running into him much at work. I saw other drivers more than I saw him. Nonetheless, Dan had Elly's affections. He'd slipped in under my radar. I'd been hoodwinked, bamboozled, shafted, fucked over!

Suddenly I was beginning to feel the stress in my life. Grade twelve wasn't going to last forever. In fact, graduation was quickly approaching. I had more than enough credits to graduate long before the year was up. People were asking what my plans were after high school. How the hell did I know? Continue working at the shitty bakery, I supposed. What else was there? I had no grand plan. Jesus, I was only eighteen. Are eighteen-year-olds really expected to know exactly what they want to do in life? Maybe some do know, but I didn't. I hadn't even thought about it. I'd been too busy thinking about Elly for the past three years, and she was with Dan!

The morning of our graduation, I snuck a twenty-dollar bill from Mom's wallet while she was still sleeping (the one and only time I ever did that). Then I borrowed Debbie's car to drive up to Delhi to pick Dwayne up. It was raining. I made it as far as Dunville, and then as I rounded a bend, the car fish-tailed out of control and I crashed into a hydro post. The car's battery was knocked out of place, causing an instant death to the engine. The post I kissed had toppled over and dented in the aluminum siding on a storage building.

As fate would have it, Mom's twenty paid off the tow truck driver for readjusting the battery for me. The Cop wrote me a ticket and I continued on my way to pick Dwayne up. Definitely put a damper on my day. I ended up having to dish out seven-hundred dollars for the repair of the building, paid a court fee of one-hundred dollars, lost a few points on my license for so-called Careless Driving, and suffered one year's suspension of my license.

But on the other hand, it made my graduation unfucking forgettable. As far as the ceremony itself, I guess I was on a personal mission to make a statement about who I was. I had a side part in my stuck-up hairdo. I couldn't afford a snazzy dress suit, so I went all Ducky. In case you were asleep during the 80's, or not born, Ducky was a poignant character in *Pretty In Pink*.

So, anyway, I wore a T-shirt under a mint-green cotton jacket, with black and white high tops. And I was so lanky, my cheekbones protruded through my sunken cheeks (I hated myself). And what I tried to pull off as ballsy was really my way of hiding. Mr. Mitler was the Master Of Ceremonies. We'd all written our future goals on skew cards for him to read off as we came up for our diplomas. I don't know what I wrote, but when I heard all the wonderful plans the other students had, my shit just didn't compare.

I found a piece of paper to write on, snuck it to Mr. Mitler, and thought I'd made a change to be proud of. But as Mitler read my card to the hundred or so parents and faculty, I didn't want to come out from behind those curtains. He read: "Michael Dube plans to pursue a career in high fashion modeling." I think my ears were bleeding. I shook Mitler's hand, smiled back at him as I looked into his very blue eyes, and wondered if he knew how insignificant I felt.

I walked off that stage without making eye contact with a single soul in the audience. Mr. East, who was there with my mother, took a picture. I sat in my designated chair and wished the day was over. High school was over. Our graduation photos were too expensive, so I just kept the proofs. And there I was, sitting in the middle of Elly and Mona in our photo together. I had cut and permed my hair into the same style as Mr. Mitler's—he'd acknowledged my attempt to mimic him. I wore a *pink* and powder-blue dress shirt, with a tie that was a darker shade of...*pink,* topped off with a... *pink* V-neck sweater. And pink says what: daring? bold? individualistic? Queer? I still didn't know.

What Did You Do With My Real Mother?

With school no longer an issue, I found myself having more time on my hands. I focused on a hobby I'd been enjoying for a couple years: writing poetry. Now, you may ask yourself, is every queer artistically inclined? YES! As a matter of fact, we are. There's a saying, "And they'll know us by our rule over the Arts." (I'm kidding!) It does seem funny to me, however, that I do fit a lot of the stereotypical notions people have about which skills queers mostly excel in. But that's just me.

Anyway, I held my job at the bakery. I think I was earning a mere three dollars and fifty cents an hour (living the dream!) At home, Tammy had moved out and into an apartment with Tim. Mom was down to just Bi and I. She suffered from migraines almost every day. I used to hear her whimper in her sleep; it was so sullen. It seemed that just as I had been clueless in the matter of Elly and Dan, I was just as unaware in matters at home—Again. For one evening, Mom solemnly approached me.

"Bi and I are moving in with Mr. East. You have about three weeks left before you have to get out of this place. They'll be coming in to clean it up for the next people," she said, hurriedly.

I couldn't believe it. Was I nothing important to anyone? How could she do this to me? I had nowhere to go. I had nothing to my name but a cheap bedroom set. I was making 3.50 and hour. Where the hell was I going to go on 3.50 an hour? And why did she wait so long to tell me? They didn't even talk to me about it.

"There's no room for you at his house," she said.

Not that I wanted to move in with Mr. East, I still hated him. But, I mean, Mom, what were you doing to me? What were you thinking by moving in with *him*? You guys were arguing every time he came over. You never got along. Three weeks? Where the hell was I going to go? The mother I knew would have never abandoned one of her kids. But that was the answer, wasn't it? She was no longer that person. This wasn't the mother I knew. She was lost to me, and lost to herself. And now I was alone.

The house echoed with emptiness when Mom and Bi left. I tried to be there as little as possible. One morning as I waited for Elly to come by to pick me up so we could walk to work together, there came a knock at the door. Expecting Elly, I opened the door and walked away. When she hadn't come in, I went back to see what she was doing outside. Much to my embarrassment and surprise, this guy with tussled blonde hair was standing there.

"I'm sorry," I said. "I'm waiting for someone and I thought you were her." I tightened the belt on my housecoat, as I was not yet dressed.

He smiled as he glanced from my bare feet back up to my eyes. "I'm doing a survey. Can I take a minute of your time?" he asked.

Well, having already made a fool of myself, I agreed to answer his question about whether or not I was *for* or *against* the death penalty in Canada. And after he thanked me for my time, I began to close the door. That's when he said, "You look pretty sexy in your housecoat."

I chuckled, continuing to close the door, when he squeezed one more question between the crack.

"Would you like a blowjob?"

My jaw dropped. My reaction was to open the door wider, look at him, then slam it shut and lock it. My heart was a ping-pong ball bouncing off the walls in my chest. Thoughts raced through my mind. I was terrified. Shocked. Grossed out. Excited. Disappointed that I didn't say yes. What was wrong with me, I wondered. That was a dream moment come true: someone offering to suck my cock. And I blew it, in a manner of speaking.

It wasn't long before Elly finally did arrive. I quickly told her about the creepy queer who'd come calling. And as I confirmed my heterosexuality, I remained secretly bitter with myself for passing on such an opportunity. In my mind I formed a collage of all the reasons my reaction had been the right one. But no matter how many rights I came up with, that one wrong could have been so good. I couldn't free myself from wondering, *What if*?

As soon as Elly and I joined Mona at the bakery, I told them about my moving dilemma. And during one of our breaks, we grabbed the newspaper and began to look through the apartment ads. To my great relief, they made the choice to move into a place with me. Apparently, their life at home was not up to par, so my misfortune was their good fortune. Mona made a couple calls right out of that very paper on that very night, and we had our very first apartment.

Come the end of that month, the three of us moved—ironically enough—into a small upper apartment on *Wallace Avenue*! Split three ways, we would each pay one-hundred and twenty dollars per month. The apartment only had two bedrooms, and really only had one bedroom, if you excluded my closet-sized space. Standing in the center of my bedroom, I could outstretch my arms and touch the opposite walls. Had I had a regular bed instead of the fold-out chair, I would not have fit it. Mona's room was small, too, but large enough for her entire bedroom set. And Elly was lucky she had a pull-out sofa to sleep on in the living room.

I remember the day Elly came home from Dan's, crying hysterically. She didn't know anyone was home. Actually, I found her behavior a little amusing; she was having a temper tantrum, mumbling incoherently, and in a childish voice. Seems Dan was jealous of her relationship with me. That's right—*I* was the reason for their break-up. She was so distraught, she even told me he was upset that she laughed at everything I said, but didn't laugh at his jokes. Hhmm. I hadn't realized I was having such an effect on their relationship, and I wasn't even trying!

I don't recollect exactly how long we occupied that apartment, but between Mona's sloppiness and this incredible feud we had with her, it wasn't meant to last. Along came Dad. He convinced me to leave Welland and move out to Florida with him. (Yeah, Florida again.) His entire life, Dad couldn't get Florida off his brain. So I broke the news to the girls, quit my job at the bakery, and waited to move with Dad. Didn't happen.

Something came up and Dad changed his mind. Couldn't change his mind before I quit my fucking job and lost the fucking apartment…no. I was so pissed at him and he didn't seem to give two shits that he'd just totally fucked me over. Elly and I went to our Landlord to explain what had transpired, but it was too late, they'd already granted the apartment to new tenants. I think they were lying about it just so we wouldn't stay. Our major feud with Mona probably didn't impress them. Nonetheless, we were out on our asses.

Mona crash-landed at a friend's house. This guy was a single older man living in a war-time house. Mona was only supposed to stay until she found another apartment, but she would end up taking advantage of her friend's kindness. And much to his chagrin, she stayed for a couple *years*! On the other side of the city, Elly and I moved in with Bev. We stuffed Elly's oversize sectional into Bev's basement, where we'd sleep. That lasted a few months, until Richard and his wife convinced me to come and live with them in Port Colborne. So I did. Elly, having no other options, landed back at her parent's house.

The High Life

For the next two years my life went up in smoke. It was a surreal time. I wish I could return. Living at Richard's was never supposed to last as long as it did. Once I got settled in, however, I didn't want to leave. Richard and Katy had two young daughters, Cherie and Brenda. I adored those kids. Brenda was probably only four-years-old and Cherie a couple years older. They had chestnut-brown hair like their mother's, and it hung down to their butts; Richard loved long hair.

(It's raining today as I'm writing. It's easy to cry for Richard on rainy days.)

He was ten years older than I—Richard. Those years had always kept us from truly knowing one another, but that was about to end. By then I was 20-years-old and Richard was thirty. I'd never smoked cigarettes or experimented with drugs, but that was about to change as well. Richard and Katy liked their Marijuana, and soon I would be liking it too. That simple little plant was a member of the family. It joined us after breakfast, during lulls in the day, in the evenings, in the car, when company came over, and it tucked us into bed at night.

Richard and I got along great. We were brothers, man. I was his 'Bro.' We were so much alike and yet so different. And our differences are what brought us closer. Dad once told me that Richard had compared him and I in this way: he was mechanically inclined and I was the one with book smarts. Be that as it was, when we were together, just the two of us, messing around in his garage, listening to Floyd or Zepplin, doping ourselves up; we were the same, and we loved each other.

That garage. He couldn't afford a real garage with concrete flooring and such, so he purchased some lumber to construct a small addition to the back of his house. The night before we were to put this thing together, he'd explained the plans to me. I don't think I had paid much attention. I was probably high. So, there we were, prepping ourselves the next day for the job ahead. The sun was shining, promising a beautiful afternoon. Katy came outside and sat on their wooden steps. She had a glass of Pepsi in her hand, as usual, and lit the neatly rolled joint she held.

The music was playing, our moods were relaxed, and it was time to construct. All I remember is staring back at Richard's bloodshot bluish-green eyes. Him and I are the only two in the family with bluish-green eyes, which turned a brighter shade of green when we were high. The rest of the family was blessed with amazingly pure blue eyes. So I gazed into Richard's eyes as he rambled on and on, placing 2x4s in a pattern on the grass. I wasn't even paying attention to his words. I just kept giggling and staring back at him. I felt so good that day. And finally, Richard stopped what he was doing, turned to look up at me and asked, "What are you laughing at?"

"You," I said.

"Well, you'd better be paying attention 'cause you're gonna have to put this together when I leave for work," he told me, smiling.

"What? You're going to work?"

Oh, shit. I had no idea he was going to leave me with the task of putting this thing together all by myself. Suddenly, I wasn't giggling anymore. This was fucking serious. I couldn't do this. How was I supposed to do this? I wasn't the hands-on guy—he was! And do you know, Richard left for work and I put that frame together as if he'd psychically implanted the instructions in my mind. I did it.

At night, while Richard was at work, Katy and I got to know one another on a deeply personal level (not the way you're thinking). The bond between us was exclusive. She was the one I confided all my secrets and desires to. She alone knew how I ached to be with Elly. She alone knew how I felt about my parents, and how I saw the world. And she alone understood the differences of opin-

ions between Richard and I. She was much more than just my sister-in-law, she was my friend, my best friend in those days.
It was while living with them that I wrote my first novella on an old typewriter Katy had. It was there that I penned my first journal and began to explore poetry from a whole new perspective. My mind opened up in that house, with my brother and his wife. I was growing up suddenly.

Whenever Elly wasn't working, she'd drive out to pick me up. I was a bad influence on her. Thanks to Richard's homegrown, we had an endless supply of pot. I'd wear this jean vest that Katy gave me. It had a tiny inner pocket, where I could hide a few pre-rolled joints to take with me for the day. Driving either her mother or her father's car, Elly and I did a lot of parking in remote areas to talk and toke. We were just enjoying each other's company, and I was so in love with her.

There were so many times when I would spill my guts to her in those cars, throwing my emotions on the dashboard for her to ingest. I'd talk and talk and she'd listen, but never would she respond to me. It was so incredibly frustrating for me. I just could not get her to open up to me. By night, she'd drop me off in Port, Richard would be gone to work, and I'd vent to Katy. It seemed to me that I was getting absolutely nowhere with Elly. I wished I didn't care. I wished I could just forget about her, but I couldn't. All the years of longing for her had come to a boil. I was obsessed with making her understand how I felt. Something had to change because I couldn't stand it anymore. I was ready to erupt. I was in love.

I don't know how much Katy shared with Richard when I wasn't around. I'm not sure what he knew about Elly and me. But right at a time when I was freaking out over my feelings for Elly, he brought something up at the dinner table I was not prepared for. Two couples who'd been hanging around as of late, invited Richard and Katy out one night. Apparently, the two woman asked my brother and his wife if I was gay. They suggested that perhaps I was and didn't know it yet. Richard, being the macho man that he was, could not let it rest without a definite answer from me.

Katy was furious with him for bringing it up at the table, in front of their daughters. I was mortified. I thought, *How the hell could those women know? I didn't act gay. My hair was long. I smoked dope. I didn't fit the stereotype. They didn't even know me. I was in love with Elly!*

I answered no to Richard, but I wasn't sure he bought it. I wasn't sure I bought it. It didn't make sense. How could I have such strong feelings for Elly, thinking of no one but her every waking moment, yet still know those secret thoughts of attraction to other men lurked in the depths of my psyche. *And how did they know, those fuckers*? I hated those people. I hated them for who they were, and I hated them for waltzing in on our lives and exposing something I wasn't ready to accept.

Shit-Hawk Island

It was a while before I could shake the defiled feeling Richard's question had left in me. Katy told me she'd tried to tell Richard not to ask me, but he was a no bullshit kind of guy. I was resentful about it, wondering how he could have the nerve to even put such a question to his brother. After all, if I was gay I would have told him, right? (Wrong.) Even now I struggle with not knowing how he would have reacted to my coming out. Would I have lost my only brother because of it? Would we have gotten into a screaming match? Would he have disowned me? Hated me? Hugged me and said it was okay? Punched me in the face? I'll never know.

Shortly after that ordeal, I think he tried to apologize Richard style. He asked me to walk down to the beach with him one evening, during sunset. His house was about a block or two from Nickel Beach. We cut through some bushes to get over to the side of the beach where the Seagulls were nesting. Shit-hawks may be gross, but you have to experience their nesting grounds at least once. Nothing less than amazing is what it was. The nests were scattered over the entire island, with a mere foot space between them. The gulls screeched so loud as we passed through their territory, our ears were ringing.

A thousand shit-hawks formed a dome overhead; it was a miracle we didn't get crapped on. We made our way through the field to the rock cliffs, where the sun was shining its final rays upon us. Richard sparked up a number and passed it to me. There was no talk about being gay or anything. We were brothers sharing a toke, sharing a private moment next to the rushing waves, the screeching gulls, and the warmth radiating off the rocks. I wish I could remember what we did talk about, but I can't.

From one moment to the next, the temperature was dipping.

Puffy-eyed and smiling, Richard turned to me and said, " Betchya can't run through the field without crushing a single egg!" He then sprinted forth, running and hopping, looking like a monkey. About a hundred feet away from me, he stopped and faced me, yelling, "You're turn!"

I had to take a moment to catch my breath from laughing about him. I felt like a student of kung fu, learning from his Master. I sucked in a breath and darted across the field. My eyes spotted the eggs to the left and right, here and there. When I reached my brother, he was laughing. We checked out each other's shoes for evidence, but we appeared to both be clean. I never attempted such a feat again. Can you imagine what the gulls must have been thinking? Probably the same thing I was: *Look at that crazy Richard.*

Apparently, Green Is Not My Color

My days with Richard were splendid, and my nights with Katy were insightful. But one night spent with both of them became frightful! You like that rhyme? Sounds like a Christmas song; but that night was anything but Joyful and Triumphant. It is most disappointing that this one experience will always stand above all other memories of my days with Richard and Katy.

It was the weekend, Friday or Saturday, I can't be certain which. I'd just spent a few days in Welland (sleeping at Mom's would be my guess). There we were, the three of us again. What should have been an average night with my brother and his wife, became something quite out-of-the-norm for them, and especially for me. It was the time of year when Richard's homegrown was in short supply. But I had arrived with a tiny brown treat in my pocket.

Having cost me my last thirty-five dollars, I'd picked up a very small chunk of hash. Just when Katy was about to roll us a fairly weak joint, I flashed my little surprise. Richard and Katy were thrilled. I know, it sounds pathetic, thrilled over a piece of hash, but they were. Funny thing is, I wasn't. I didn't mind giving it to them because I really didn't like hash. Being the miniscule chunk that it was, Katy made the suggestion that we retire upstairs and smoke it between hot knives. Richard agreed. And me, well, I remember smiling, and hating the thought of it. *Me and my stupid chunk of hash.*

I followed them upstairs, where they had a very small wreck room, a washroom, and their bedroom. Richard's stereo was up there, a small television set, a loveseat, and my bed over in an off-section of the room, neatly squeezed into its place. Someone turned on the radio as Richard dug out his little propane tank, and a magazine already left prepped for the job of cone-pipe. (All that means is that Richard had rolled a magazine up in the shape of a cone and taped it to remain that way.)

Together, he and Katy sat on the carpeted floor and lit the torch. Richard diced the hash into tiny specks, which looked like pepper to me. Since I'd brought the stuff, they let me go first. I held the cone over the smoke as Richard burned the hash between two butter knives. Taking a deep breath in, I inhaled the fumes, my lips covering the smaller end of the cone. I did this three times, then handed the cone to Katy. I'd only smoked hash in this manner once before, and this second round appeared to be an almost exact enactment of that first time.

I went first, Katy second, and Richard last. Only, by the time it was Richard's turn, he and Katy wound up arguing about how she wasn't burning the hash properly or something. They did this both times I was with them. I remember thinking that maybe Richard didn't like knife-tokes any more than I did, and that this was his way to screw it up for himself. I couldn't see what she was doing that was so aggravating for him. But I watched, and I listened, and something was wrong…with me.

Richard sat at the opposite end of the sofa from me. He and Katy were finished with the tokes, but continued to nag each other. Meanwhile, I was tuned out of their conversation, listening to the loudness of my heartbeat in my ears. I crossed my arms and sat silent, losing my breath as beats beneath my right hand pummeled against my palm. This wasn't the same pulse I'd felt stepping up onto the stripper stage for the fashion show. That was exhilarating, while this besieged me with panic.

I heard Richard say my name, but I didn't respond the first time. Then he reached to grab my left arm. I turned to look at him. "Holy shit, Mike! Are you okay? You look…*greeeen*!" he said, his eyes wild.

I finally found the will to speak, and replied, "I can't breathe."

Richard and Katy leapt to their feet at once. Richard put his arm under mine and raised me off of the sofa. Not four steps down the staircase, I was suddenly dangling from his hold, my legs melting beneath me. He led me out onto their porch and down to their picnic table. The air was chilly and stars appeared as nothing more than needle-points in the clear night sky. I took deep breaths, feeling a boost of reassurance from the moments of clarity that swept through my thoughts.

"Are you okay? Can you breathe?" Richard kept asking as he danced nervously around me.

"Just take him to the hospital," Katy suggested. "Don't take any chances."

The last thing my brother wanted to do was take me to the hospital in my condition, or in *his*. We were stoned, man. What would they think? We knew what they would think—we were stoners. Can't imagine what would give them that idea. There I was: tall and lanky, a hundred and eighteen pounds, muscle shirt on, shorts, my hair grown out to match Bono's during the *Joshua Tree Tour*, and my right shoulder donning the rose tattoo Richard had paid his friend to ink for my eighteenth birthday.

While they argued, hospital or no, all I could think was that if I could sing, I could breathe. "What do you want me to do, Mike? Do you want me to drive you to the hospital?" Richard asked. I shook my head. His fears were my fears. I didn't want to go to the hospital. "Well, what do you want to do?"

"I want to sing," I said.

"What?"

"I want to sing," I repeated, breaking into a song.

Richard didn't get it. They were freaking out and I wanted to *sing*!

"Doesn't matter what he says," Katy went on. "Just get him to the fucking hospital, you idiot!"

"He said he doesn't want to go. It's just a bad trip," Richard insisted.

"How do you know it's just a bad trip? What if he gets worse?"

"Mike, do you want me to take you to the hospital, man?" Richard asked me again, staring me in the face.

This time I nodded. The singing was no longer doing the trick; I couldn't breathe anymore. I couldn't stand.

"See!" Katy said, frustrated. "He wants to go!"

Even once we were seated in his car, Richard kept asking me if I was positive I wanted him to bring me to the hospital. Rocking back and forth, I'd tell him no, then tell him yes. His indecisiveness was confusing me. Finally, we drove away from their house and made it up to the main bridge, before he stopped the car to question me about it further.

"Are you sure you wanna go? I can't go in with you. Not in the state I'm in. They'll call the cops. Are you sure you wanna go?" he rambled.

Cops? I thought. *They won't call the cops...will they*?

It made no difference. I could feel things happening inside my body that were scaring me far more than the chance of police involvement. I had to go. I needed help. We drove on until we entered the hospital parking lot. And even then, Richard kept asking if I was absolutely certain I didn't want to change my mind. I assured him that I was going in, and that I was all right without him at my side.

He pulled up to the emergency doors, where I stepped out of the car. I don't remember what he said before I shut the door and he slowly drove away, looking back at me with angst. We were acting like a couple criminals, and I was the one shot during our fumbled escape, now having no choice but to turn myself in on account of my life-threatening injuries.

There I was at a strange hospital, standing outside glass doors, and unable to figure out how the hell to get in. A young man (a nurse) finally helped me inside. I immediately told him I needed to see a doctor. He led me passed the reception desk and into a room. I was trembling uncontrollably as he began to ask me questions about what I might have taken to cause the reaction I was having.

Teeth ground together as speaking was difficult, I lied, exaggerating, when I said, "I smoked...a joint...of hash."

He ran down a long list of drugs, as if he hadn't heard my first answer. "I...smoked...a...joint...of...hash," I repeated, my voice full of anger because I knew he didn't believe me.

The young nurse was actually very soft-spoken and gentle with me, as I recall. The moment he wrapped the cuff of a sphygmomanometer (blood pressure cuff) around my arm and pumped it up, my entire body shook. I was quick to take in more deep breaths, trying to control the spasms.

"Good," the nurse said. "Just keep inhaling." He removed the cuff, much to my relief, and headed out of the room, saying, "I'll be right back. Just sit still and keep taking deep breaths."

All I could think about was how pathetic I must have appeared. I was humiliated and helpless. The nurse returned and led me to a second room, where he asked me to lie down on the bed. Once I laid back, he removed my sandals and disappeared for another moment. Then it was my body's turn to display its anger, anger with me. And, man, I never knew how pissed off one's body could get.

First I began to have convulsions. My body was literally bouncing off that bed. I couldn't stop it, and I was terrified. Every part of me was out of my control. I looked down at my chest, which seemed to have inflated so much so that I couldn't see past it to my feet. I could feel the muscles in my chest spreading and tearing, and all the while I was shaking. The male nurse was suddenly standing at the foot of my bed with a female nurse. I couldn't hear what they were saying, but I saw the male nurse touch the undersides of my flexed feet with a silver prong. I guessed he was trying to trigger a relaxing response. The attempt failed.

Then a third nurse came into the room. She was impatiently struggling to attach those sticky suction cups to different parts of my chest. Of course, I was convulsing so much, the suctions kept popping off. "Try to hold still," she said with annoyance in her voice.

"I…am…trying," I grunted back.

She eventually got the little suckers to stick, started her machine up, and walked away. I turned my head to watch the needles erratically sketching my equally erratic pulse rate. I didn't need a machine to calculate the beats-per-minute; I could feel my heart raging inside of me, galloping its way to some unknown finish-line. It seemed that as the machine buzzed away, my convulsions increased. I don't even remember the nurse returning to remove the suctions. But again I found myself alone in the very bright room, waiting for my body's next assault.

I thought I was going to die. Then, all of a sudden, in the midst of my private earthquake, I felt like my body dropped from the sky and landed with a great wallop onto the bed. And I was a rock. I couldn't move a single part of my being. I was locked down, as if that old grade-school dumpster had been thrown on top of me once more to remind me how stupid I'd been. I was paralyzed.

I felt something like an egg crack upon the center of my chest; and I felt its innards spreading across my skin in all directions (still paralyzed). Then Katy appeared just outside my room, where I heard her speaking with a doctor. Though I hadn't even been examined by him, he was telling her that he suspected I had overdosed on heroin or cocaine. Katy shook her head, insisting that she knew me very well, and that I would most certainly not have tried any such drugs.

A single moment before she came to stand at my bedside, I felt the chains of punishment unlock. My vengeful body suddenly released its grasp and I slipped into ease, loosening up, and breathing a sigh of relief. Katy hunched over me, her face pale from fear.

"Mike," she whispered, "are you okay? They think you did some heavy drugs, you know?"

"Just before you came in, I couldn't even move," I told her. "And that one nurse fucking pissed me off."

"What happened? What did they do for you?" she went on.

"Fuck all!" I said as the suction-cup nurse returned. She placed a tiny pill under my tongue and told me to relax for a few moments.

"What did you give him?" asked Katy.

"Nitroglycerin," the nurse answered.

After the nurse walked out, Katy looked at me and said, "Holy shit. They give that to people having heart-attacks."

I didn't know exactly what the fuck had just happened to me, but the hospital allowed Katy to take me home about twenty minutes later. I couldn't believe they were letting me leave. *That's it*? I thought *I almost die and they let me go home*? I couldn't understand it, and I really didn't care. I was more than glad to leave and return to Richard's. On the way home, Katy told me how angry she was at Richard for having dumped me at the hospital and gone back home.

"Are you fucking nuts?" she'd asked him. "You don't even know what's happening to him, you goof."

Richard looked just like my sad-eyed-puppy-picture when we arrived home. The whole thing had scared him so much, he told me he'd even sworn to GOD that if He'd let me be okay, he wouldn't smoke ever again. Of course, he broke that promise almost at once. But at least he was sincere in his heart. As Katy disappeared upstairs to run a bath for me, Richard and I sat on the sofa downstairs. He just gazed at me as I continued to suffer body spasms. But once I sank into the warmth of the bath, I couldn't believe I was alive. It had been one *hell* of a night.

Unknown to Richard and Katy, I would live with the scars for years to come. Whatever had gone wrong, my body wasn't about to let me forget so soon. Pain in my chest resisted healing. I couldn't lie back in the bathtub the way I normally did to wash my hair or relax; the strain at my chest was excruciating. Nor could I lean far forward, for the same pain befell me. And hugs, well, ask my mother how long it was before she could hug me without having me groan. Any slight pressure on my chest was too much pressure.

And it wasn't just my chest that was suffering long. I was drained, physically and mentally. I tried to be okay but it was a losing battle. I remember how Elly would pick me up and spend entire days with me, driving the two of us around to isolated locations. I couldn't stand to be around anyone. I'd been beaten down and left for a vegetable. Elly was so good to me in those days, always at my side, bearing my unbearable company. She listened to my endless whining about the pain in my left temple—a pinprick. This invisible pin pierced into my brain with sudden ferocity, and at any given moment. I never knew what it was.

Worse than all the suffering was still my stupidity. Perhaps the seizure had taken more than its share of brain cells. For I continued to toke with Elly until my supply was gone. (Now *that's* stupid!) No one else in the family knew what I'd experienced. It was a secret between Rich, Katy, Elly, and myself. What I couldn't understand was how the rest of the family, especially my mother, was kept unaware. I looked like a corpse. I was withdrawn. I felt like someone had switched my body for that of an eighty-year-old! I spent what was left of that summer moving about as if in a daydream.

It became difficult for me to be around Rich and Katy. Simply because they were still smoking pot. My new body reacted to the smoke in the air like the antennas of a snail, withdrawing instantly—instinctively. My pulse would jump into hyper-drive at once. On one occasion, Richard even tried to coax me into sharing a pipe toke with him...of hash! I couldn't believe he'd asked me. *You want to kill me*? I thought. He didn't realize just how severe my attack of that night had been. So I began to withdraw from him, coming around much less.

Eventually, my hell night would be exposed to the rest of the family. This exposure came about because it appeared that I was not the only stupid member. Turned out, Beverly had suffered an allergic reaction to hash at her boyfriend's house one evening. Her experience wasn't quite as dramatic as mine had been, but it taught her to stay clear of drugs in a hurry. Tammy, on the other hand, suffered a much worse reaction than both of us.

Her stupidity landed her in the back seat of Mom's car, on the floor, *dead* no less. For about three minutes she was a corpse. If my mother hadn't arrived at the hospital with her when she did, the doctor said they wouldn't have been able to revive her. I must not have seen much of Tammy during that period because I don't recall how her recovery went. Guess I was too busy being my own outpatient. With allergies to just about everything running rabid in our family, you would have thought we'd be smart enough to stay clear of life's temptations.

The letters

Since my days living at Richard's were winding down, I'd begun to spend more nights sleeping at Mom's. Not Mr. East's, but Mom's. Things had not worked well living with Mr. East, so she and Bi had moved into an apartment, down the street from Elly's house. Of course, in no time at all, he'd come pleading to Mom to come back to him, and she would. This was the first of nine moves in and out of his house that Mom would make. NINE! The ninth being as recent as present day, 2008.

In my own fucked-up relationship, with all of my efforts to convince Elly that she and I were meant to be together, I'd only succeeded in stealing a single kiss from her. It happened one night in Richard's driveway. Elly was dropping me off and I asked her for a goodnight kiss. She hesitated, then leaned in and gave me a quick peck on the lips.

"That's it?" I said. "After all we've been through, that's the best you can do?"

"It feels weird," she said.

I was insulted. I got out of the car and didn't turn back to watch her drive away. Katy was home alone, so I walked in and immediately told her about the lousy kiss. Man, there I was in my twenties and still a freaking virgin! Elly wasn't. Dan had seen to that. I was becoming a miserable man. I hated my life. Hated the job I had working midnights in a shitty Niagara Falls convenient store. I was tired of feeling like I was wasting my energy on Elly, and losing touch with my inner peace. I was angry all the time.

Then Dad came down from up north, where he'd purchased some property at Bear Lake. He and I chatted about all things miserable, and out of that conversation, we'd agreed that I would move up to his house. Richard was envious of me, being the outdoorsman that he was. The rest of the family, however, was not pleased with the prospect of not having me around them. And Elly, not one for words as I had learned, planted a juicy kiss on me the day I was leaving. I was flabbergasted.

So what was that? I remember wondering. *A great goodbye kiss, or a please* **don't go kiss**? I didn't ask.

Off I went. I could feel the stress I'd been storing up begin to slip away as Dad and I drove up north. I didn't actually move into his house. I moved into our old bus, which was now nestled in with the trees at the far end of Dad's property. Without anything to distract me, my head felt unclouded for the first time in a long time. I went right to work on my novel, scribbling all night long and sleeping all day. It was bliss. I was living out my Jack Kerouac fantasy—freedom and writing.

When I wasn't writing, I passed the time running from dump sight to dump sight with Dad's live-in third cousin, Milia. She was an odd little woman, with two young daughters. She had a couple sons, too, but they still lived in the State of Maine, where Dad had picked her and the girls up. He'd lived there for a year or two with Richard, Katy, and baby Cherie. This was after the whole kidnapping fiasco.

When I wasn't with Milia, I would take long walks on the path behind our property. It was gorgeous out there. I was sure to spot deer with every walk. The tranquil strolls afforded me the time I needed to refocus on my book and catch my breath. I was feeling a hundred percent finer than I did back home. I was eating with Dad and Milia every day, unafraid to fill myself up. I had no responsibilities. Dad expected nothing from me. He was content just to have me. And for the first time since I could not remember, I myself was content.

For more than two years I lived up at Dad's, writing and growing. I traveled back and forth from Bear Lake to Welland, countless times. Mostly, I preferred to stay at the lake. Dad was still healthy in those days, still dabbling in real estate. He didn't know how to sit still. He couldn't even seem to enjoy his own property. His first love was always being on the go. The winters were fantastic up there. It was dry, unlike the dampness that Welland winters carry with them. The snow was knee-deep, the air crisp, and the night sky spectacular. Besides the heat, I don't know what Dad ever thought Florida could give him that the north couldn't.

Letters from my family began to arrive. You can imagine what that was like. I felt like a movie star replying to fan mail. But I loved getting their letters because I loved writing back. A pen may as well have been stitched to my hand, for all the time it spent there. Letters and cards came for Dad as well, but he didn't bother with them. I'd find unopened cards from my sisters strewn about in his van. There were even photos of their children in those cards, so I kept them all. He was such a loving man, this father I'd come to appreciate, so why didn't he care about his daughters? I couldn't figure him out.

He and Milia began to pay visits to me in the bus, interrupting my better moments of writing, as if they knew I was on a roll. She'd come in and complain about him; he'd come in and blow off steam about her. I found it all quite amusing. Of course, I had to remain neutral in any advice or comments I would make. Basically, I think they just needed my ears and not my opinions anyway. I loved them both dearly.

Eventually, Richard and my sisters came up during the summer. We had wonderful times. Richard and I even slept on the lakeshore one night. There was a warm, gentle breeze we just couldn't resist. Richard was surprised that I wanted to sleep by the lake (guess I didn't strike him as the outdoor type). As we lay side by side in our sleeping bags, I quickly fell asleep to the hushing of the waves and wind. The next morning, I awoke to Richard's smiling face.

"Haven't the flies been bothering you?" he asked.

"What flies?" I said. "Your bad breath must've attracted them."

We enjoyed an amazing summer. Richard led us on a hike through the bush one afternoon, until we happened upon a beautiful river. It was so hot, Katy was the first to attempt a dip in the river. She was searching for a safe entrance, while Richard and I explored the waterfall. I took my shoes off and carefully climbed down into the cradle of the falls, where the rocks formed a perfect seat. The water was replenishing and warm, and soon everyone was joining me: Rich, Katy, Elly, and Mona. My nieces: TammyJeanne, Cherrie, and Brenda. My nephew, Jesse. And Bev, who was pregnant for Julie.

Rich and I even skinny-dipped out at a small island under the night sky. We'd named the island Toker's Point, for obvious reasons. Bev and Katy had canoed there with us but neither of them went swimming. I remember how warm the surface water was, and how Rich and I both saw a brilliant shooting-star that the girls missed because it had appeared behind their backs, as if it was meant for his and my eyes alone. We were so excited about the star, the girls thought we were bullshitting them. The next day, Rich and I went out in the canoe again and traced the entire lake. I felt limitless love for my brother that precious, precious summer.

During my second winter at Dad's, my mother and sisters began to question how much longer I was planning to stay away. They were missing me, but I wasn't ready yet. The letters continued to come in, and I continued to answer them right back. I didn't return to Welland for Christmas. I'd moved myself out of the bus—it was a giant icebox. Now I was in one of those tiny campers that sit on the back of a pickup truck. Yeah, I was moving up in the world. Dad hated me being in there. Every day he'd beg me to move into the small cottage with him, Milia, and the two girls. He couldn't believe that I was hot in my camper bed, but I was—sweating.

I had a small table placed in the corner, right next to the door. A thick sheet of ice had built up on the inside wall, from the ceiling to the floor, right behind my table. So as I wrote, I was staring at ice. No wonder Dad couldn't believe I was warm in there. But a tiny space-heater threw its heat directly up to my bed, where it remained trapped. I actually had to open the small window at my head to let fresh air in, and was still too hot!

I remember complaining to Dad that for some reason I wasn't dreaming in that camper. He advised me to imagine the window as a portal for which my dream spirit could escape (sounds funny but it worked!) I wasn't sleeping alone, either. I had a feline visitor to keep me company. Don't know who he belonged to, but every night he came to my door to get out of the cold. He'd meow to be let out the next morning, and I wouldn't see that cat all day.

There's something I like about letting time pass before coming back to people. I like it when they can see the changes in you. As if you'd become a better person than the one they'd last seen. Or, in my case, maybe just a hairier person. So, it was no wonder I allowed myself a certain amount of time between my Welland visits. It was important for me to feel like I'd accomplished something with my writing, had something I could speak of, and not seem as if I'd been doing nothing.

Sometimes the minute I returned to Dad's, I would seclude myself from Milia and her girls to write letters. Although I had only just left my sisters and Elly, I thought of many things I wanted to tell them on the drive up. I was truly missing Richard and Katy. I'd gone from living with them to never seeing them at all. And, so, I wrote my letters: I wrote Katy to tell her how the writing was coming along; I wrote Debbie to tell her how spiritual I felt; I wrote Tammy to tell her I missed her and guessed the sex of her unborn baby; I wrote Bi to gossip about the others; I wrote Mom from the heart; I wrote Bev to remind her how much I loved her; and I wrote Elly…to ask her to marry me!

34 And Gone

The suspense of Elly's reply was killing me, so I phoned her before she could send a written response. Dad didn't have a phone for some reason (I used the pay phone across the street). Elly described to me what her mother and her mother's friend, Lil, had said to her about me. She'd gone outside to tell her mother the news about us—of course, she said yes—but the minute my name came up, her mother commented that she shouldn't get mixed up with someone like me, someone with a heart condition. I'd been diagnosed with a common condition called Mitral Valve Prolapse (Paroxysmal tachycardia) a heart murmur, basically. Lil readily agreed with Elly's mother, adding that I wasn't a good person.

Amidst a borage of insults to her future son-in-law, Elly's mother got an in-your-face "We're getting married!" Man, was I amused. Her old lady hated me the second she laid eyes upon me, and that was during tenth grade! And I'll tell ya, my relationship with Elly's mother would never improve. She wasn't the sort of woman to pretend she liked you. She threw insults my way and disagreed with every word I'd say every chance she got. I would keep my visits to her house to a minimum of Christmas and maybe one other holiday during the years. That was too many visits.
Despite her mother's greatest attempts to spew hatred upon me, I didn't care. I wasn't marrying her, I was marrying her daughter. Can't say I ever doubted it would come to pass. Can't say I ever thought it wouldn't last, either—but that came later. For now, we were getting married. Mom and Bev donated Elly's engagement ring. It wasn't a cheap ring; Bev had chosen it herself with one of her boyfriends. I didn't feel that great about it, but I used it anyway, handing it in a box to Elly in a shopping center. Not the most romantic approach. I suppose my feelings about the ring not having

come from me personally stole the romance out of it. Elly never questioned me about the ring, but I knew she had probably guessed it'd been a gift from my family. After all, I wasn't, nor had I been, working for quite some time.

Mona wasn't backing us up much. I think her never-ending jealousy of Elly got in the way. Elly still used her for a maid of honor. I had called on my best friend of all time, Dwayne, to be my best man. Too bad he wasn't able to make it down for some reason. Once again, fate stepped in and Richard filled the shoes of my best man. He appears in all of our wedding photos. I wasn't the only member of our family whose best man stiffed him. Richard's best man had done the same thing to him. Guess we weren't very lucky in the best man department. However, I think I had my best man.

On September 29 1990, Michael took Elly to be his lawfully wedded wife, and Elly took Michael to be her lawfully wedded husband. We didn't go on a honeymoon. Mom gave us her apartment for the night. (How cheesy was that?) Do you want to hear something even more pathetic? We didn't consummate the marriage that night. Elly was in her time of the month, so I respected that; also, that was gross. We opened our gifts, read our cards, calculated the money gifts, then we relaxed by soaking in Mom's tub together. That was our wedding night.

Elly had quit the bakery to marry me. I moved her up north into the house-trailer I was now living in. I was twenty-two and she was twenty-three. When she tried to collect her unemployment, the government gave her a difficult go of it. They said she didn't have a good enough reason for quitting her job. I suppose getting married and moving four hours away wasn't a good enough reason—HELLO! I don't think she ever did receive a cheque while we were up there.

Finally, after waiting a couple weeks, I made my move in the bedroom. It was again difficult to get Elly to participate. I remember telling her, frustrated, to quit acting like a virgin. (You can see I was still annoyed with the fact that Elly had given herself to Dan before giving herself to me.) I had to take her hand and place it myself on my aching erection. All my years of wanting her had brought us to this night. There was no four-play. I was so anxious to fuck, I mounted her, fumbled my way inside of her, and instantly came.

Looking back on it now, the disappointment of that night foretold the way our sex life would play out for the years to come. But I know that even had we been sexually active prior to our marriage, and it wasn't great; I was so in love, I think I would have proposed to her anyway. I've learned something incredibly important over the past year: love isn't sex and sex isn't love. You can't choose who you'll fall in love with. I loved my wife.

We had our first Christmas as man and wife at Bear Lake. Little did I know, however, that Elly was unhappy with our location. She neglected to share with me the fact that she was greatly missing her family, and wanted to return to Welland. I found out when I came across an unfinished letter she was writing to her mother. I wasn't angry. I was sad that she hadn't told me. It was okay to miss your family. It was okay to not like living up north. And I was okay with returning to Welland. (I was ready now.)

We took a one bedroom apartment on Lyons Avenue—just two streets up from Wallace. A couple we knew was living in one of the upper apartments; it was a 4-plex. Since we were both unemployed, we decided to enroll at the city college for a two year stretch. We had some rough times while living there, arguing a lot. Most of our arguments were about how much time she was spending with her mother and how little she was spending with me. And I was spending too much time writing.

I wrote two novels, one after the other in that apartment. Thought they were the most important things in my life. Richard called me up while I was writing. He asked me if I wanted to come over to be his sparring partner that afternoon. I told him I couldn't because I was too busy writing. I was too busy writing. I was too busy writing. *Goddamn me*...I was too busy WRITING?!

The following week, Elly and I were playing cards with Mona in our kitchen. We used to play cards a lot. The phone rang and I was the one to answer it. Beverly was at the other end, sobbing. "Mike?"

"Bev? What's wrong?"

"Mike, it's Richard."

"What about him?"

"He got stung by a bee."

"So," I said, not understanding the significance of what she was revealing to me.

"He didn't make it."

"What? What do you mean, he didn't make it?"

"He's gone, Mike. Our brother's gone."

At 34-years-old, my brother had died from a single bee sting. And there I was again, as I'd found myself so many times, left in the loop. Apparently, Richard's job was at an end. He and Katy were in the process of moving themselves and their girls up to Dad's. They were going to run the small gas-bar and restaurant with him. Dad had recently snagged himself the business across the street from his house. The same business where I'd stood at the phone booth so many times, talking to Richard and Katy. Richard had driven himself and the girls up ahead of Katy. In fact, she was on her way up there when he died. How devastated she must have been upon arriving at Dad's, only to learn that her husband was lying dead in the Huntsville Hospital.

It would be three days until Richard's body was brought back to Welland for his funeral. For three days I didn't cry, didn't shed a tear. I was numbed by disbelief. Three days and then…I rushed ahead of Elly into the funeral parlor. Katy was standing beside the open casket. Not five feet from where he lay, I doubled over with one hand over my chest and the other covering my gaping mouth. Katy reached to grab me and stop me from collapsing.

Oh, my god, I thought. *It's for real. It's really him. He's dead. That's really Richard in there.* And that was the moment I finally wept for my brother.

I wept for him and I wept for him. All my nights were exhausted with my weeping for him as I lie in bed. So many things bulldoze their way through your thoughts during periods of mourning. I felt cold and empty. I felt ripped off. I felt off balance by not having our brother at the other end of the family chain. I wept because he would never know my children that were as yet unborn, and my children would never know him. And I wept. And I couldn't stop thinking about that last phone call from him. *Goddamn me.*

Never again would I see him smile or hear his laughter. I would never be able to tell him I love him. I would never ride in a canoe with him. I would never be able to argue with him, or hike with him, or hunt with him, or reminisce with him, or watch him grow gray-haired. So I wept, and I wept, and I wept for him, and I wept some more. *(I continue to weep for you, Richard.)*

When Healing Is Welcome

Richard was taken from us during the summer before my second year of college was to commence. I walked about in an angry state for months, hating everything. I had zero tolerance for people in general. And then I had to go back to school. I wasn't certain how I was going to handle being at school. Nothing felt important to me. I can't even recall what classes I had, except for one: Human Relations. The Professor was an average-looking man, perhaps in his late thirties-early forties. I found we locked eyes often. I liked him and enjoyed his class. During one period, he even sat in the chair next to me for the duration of the lesson.

For our final assignment in his class, we were given the option to write an essay or give a verbal speech. To my wonder, only one other student aside from myself chose to give a speech. I believe I gave it on the inner turmoil I was suffering and how it effected me. I spoke directly to the Professor, and I could see the compassion on his face. I wish I would have thanked him for what his class had done for me. It set me on the path to healing. I had been so utterly and completely sad. Yet, and don't ask me how, my grades for that second year were much higher than they had been for the previous year. Ask the experts, I guess. Wait a minute. Maybe I do know the reason. Maybe it was because nothing whatsoever had distracted me from the actual work. I shut out the world and was able to focus on the work set before me. Could it be?

Grades or no grades, no job came to either Elly or myself from those two expensive years. We had to file for bankruptcy because of it. Under the same Landlord, we moved out of the 4-plex and into a cardboard box of a house on Churchill Street. Through her mother, Elly took work at another bakery in Font Hill. It wasn't full time so we were collecting assistance. I wasn't looking for anything. I had no ambition. I was in a rut. I was hurting and searching.

I wrote a lot of poetry dedicated to Richard. None of the poems were a success to me. I didn't feel like they were saying what I wanted them to say. I needed for the words to explode for me, and they weren't. So I kept on trying. I didn't realize at that time how much the poems *were* helping me. With each new work, I was letting go of my pain. Though no explosions happened for me, I believe each poem let out a loud cry. On September 9 1992, I jotted down the following poem:

<u>WEPT</u>

(I was folding back the sheets, humming to myself, when I suddenly realized I hadn't stopped to cry for you today. So I fell to my knees, and all it took was to think of your name...*Richard*.)

As part of my healing process, I made up my mind that it was time for Elly and I to start a family, and she agreed. We already had a spare room to accommodate a baby. All we needed was the baby. A total of 17 months would pass before our *babies* were born. Although it took many months of trying to get pregnant, Elly and I produced a set of fraternal twin girls. Knowing that our Churchill residence was too small for the four of us, in addition to the fact that mildew on the walls caused me great sickness during the winter months, we abandoned the house and moved into a townhouse, next door to Mona and her boyfriend, Tate.

Mona and Tate were already pregnant, but as of yet, unwed. Both of us unemployed, Tate and I became card-playing buddies. Every night, till the wee hours of morning, he and I played and talked. There were often nights when the four of us played cards, but mostly Tate and I were without the women. This gave us the opportunity to complain about our sex lives with the sisters, or lack of. We found the girls had much in common, as did we.

Tate came into my life at precisely the right time. His little quirks and habits reminded me so much of Richard. It wasn't in his physical appearance, but in his mannerisms. I couldn't get enough of his company; he was filling the void Richard had left.

Mona, I think, was a bit jealous. I don't know what it is with her. We'd catch her sitting on the staircase, listening in on our conversations. And the instant Tate stepped foot into our house, the phone would ring, and we knew it was her. Our door hadn't even sealed shut yet, and the phone was ringing.

She and Tate tied the knot before their son was born. And a couple months later, our twin girls, Taylor Dawn and Randee Rose, were born on May 11 1994. And oh my GOD, were they adorable! Though Elly's eyes were brown, the twin's took from my side of the family and had the bluest eyes. They were two of the most beautiful babies I'd ever seen. And I'm not just tooting my own family horn. They were gorgeous. However, there was that minor detail: they were both girls.

Elly and I had heard that following childbirth the chance of conception was greater. We didn't want to wait the length of time we'd suffered through for the first pregnancy; plus, we wanted a son. So we went to work. Meanwhile, my grandfather, on my father's side, was dieing from cancer. He had vowed to stay alive until he was able to see the twins, and he did just that. I wasn't close to my grandfather, but Richard was. And the strange thing is that one day when Rich and I were talking about Grampa's impending death, Richard told me he would rather go before Gramps, than to see him die. Life is full of coincidences like that. Even shitty coincidences.

About a year after the birth of our twins, on May 26 1995, Hunter Richard was born. His eyes sparkled blue as well, but he resembled Elly's father to an almost insane degree. Just as she had with the twins, Elly breastfed Hunter. His attachment to her left me unable to embrace my new baby. I was a stranger to Hunter for the first month or so. He wanted nothing to do with me. It was very difficult on me. I even recall feeling resentment toward the little guy. But once that phase passed, Hunter became my son.

SECURITY SUCKS

WE WEREN'T THE ONLY ONES building a family in those days. Mona and Tate had given birth to their second child, a sister for their son. Tate had taken a delivery job and I had been hired by a janitorial company. I had to drive out to Niagara Falls, St. Catharines, and other locations to perform my custodial duties. I hated it, I liked it, and then I really hated it. Without any special skills, my job choices were limited. And that's when I found a job that didn't require any special skills: security guard.

I would soon be sent all over the Niagara area to different locations, for different amounts of time, and meet different people. The small group of other security guards I would meet over the next couple years all carried the same attitude about the job as I did: it was corny. We were all just 'between' jobs. No one wanted to do this for the rest of their lives. We were glorified property sitters. Yet, I found most people I came in contact with treated me with the outmost respect. I think it's that whole authority thing. People are trained to behave a certain way around authority, no matter how lame that authority figure may be.

Some of my earlier assignments sucked pretty bad. I froze my ass off at quite a few. I hated the locations that required two guards. You never knew what loser you were going to spend eight hours twiddling your thumbs with. I met a couple descent people, but I always preferred the company of myself. For over a year I had to drive out of town to a refractory plant, where they made brick. There were only a handful of workers left, dreading the plant's imminent closure. I met one particular man on his last days before retirement.

Al was of average height and weight, with gray hair and deep blue eyes. He reminded me of a television actor, whose name eludes me. He and I spent a lot of time chatting. I got to know him pretty well during his final days. He and the other workers had expressed their dislike of my fellow guards, stating that none of them were friendly like I was. No wonder they all gathered around me when I arrived. They'd have their say, catching me up on plant news and laying their disappointments on me, then leave. And that's about when Al would come in, his face aglow from sweat, wearing his dirty coveralls, which were always unzipped down to his waist to reveal a chest covered in mostly gray hair.

I looked forward to seeing him every night. His stories were entertaining. The more I got to know him, the less he reminded me of the television actor and became more of his own person to me. His obvious years over me would eventually disperse as well. Al's voice was convincing as a young man, and I'm not referring to its tone, I'm referring to his personality. I began to find him more attractive. Not in the sense that I fantasized about a sexual encounter between us; but in a true friendship way.

When I knew his last day had come, I brought a retirement card in for him. He was genuinely appreciative. I missed him for a long time, especially since I was now completely alone in this enormous tin can. Talk about long nights. My shifts ran from midnight till noon the next day. I watched TV, ate, showered, roamed the entire property, including the rooftop—hell, I slept on the rooftop! The best part about that job was that it enabled me to write another novel.

Not Again!

It was about that time that Elly and I decided we were ready to have another child. Finding space in our lives to work on having a baby was another story. Hunter was still getting up during the night to sneak into our bed. I remember him walking in on us one night; good thing there was a pillow in my reach. He didn't notice. Once again we were living next door to Mona and Tate. It was a different set of townhouses in another part of the city. The night we went to tell them that Elly was pregnant, Mona's response took us by surprise.

The four of us were sitting at their dining room table, when Elly broke the news. Mona smacked her hand down on the table and ran up to her room. Tate shook his head as he explained to us that she'd been bugging him to have another baby. He didn't want another baby. He figured they were already struggling as it was. Elly was hurt. My family celebrated the news of another baby in our future, where as her one and only sister couldn't even congratulate her. And within a month or so, Mona was pregnant.

I was visiting at Bev's house when Elly returned from her first ultrasound. She looked a bit flushed, I thought, and it was no wonder. The ultrasound had revealed not one fetus—but two!—Again! My initial thought was that she was bullshitting me, trying to pull a fast one. When I realized this wasn't a joke, my next thought was, *Can we handle another set of twins*? *Five kids*? Elly had once said that she wanted to have five kids, but that number wasn't in my plans.

For about three or four weeks, Elly and I carried around the notion that we were about to be thrown into parent hell. Mentally, physically, financially...could we cope? Neither one of us knew. And for the three or four weeks leading up to Elly's next ultrasound appointment, she had spotting. Everyone assured us that it was normal to have spotting during the first weeks of pregnancy. But it certainly wasn't the norm for Elly's pregnancies.

While she was off for the ultrasound, I was off to visit at Bev's again. We waited anxiously for Elly's return. And when at last she walked into the house, her face appeared just as flushed as it had after her first visit.

"Well?" I said. "What'd they say this time?"

Elly sat down. "There's only one now."

"What? One? Well, what happened to the other one?" asked Bev.

Elly explained how the nurse showed her the fetus' heartbeat on the monitor, but didn't mention a second fetus. So Elly said, "What about the other baby?" She said the nurse looked at her like she was crazy.

"What other baby? There's only one."

"The last time I came the nurse showed me a second baby in its own sac," Elly told her.

"Well, it must've gotten rid of itself. Sometimes when there's a problem the fetus won't make it."

No matter what the explanation, we were now down to having one baby. It was a strange feeling. I don't know how Elly felt, but I was a little sad...for about a minute, then I was fucking jumping for joy. ONE—one baby was enough. And on October 6 1999, that's what we had—one baby girl named Chanel Sarah. (My baby girl.)

Mona wasn't as fortunate as Elly in having all natural births, without any difficulties. Her third child, like the previous two, was born by cesarean section, and had spinal meningitis. She would spend the next month in a Toronto hospital with him. Elly and I were no longer Mona and Tate's neighbors; we'd switched from our three bedroom unit to a four bedroom, around the bend. It was a much larger unit, with two washrooms and a finished basement that would later serve to increase our finances.

A New Direction

The security company I'd been employed by was slowly downsizing. Yeah, they would continue to downsize until they completely disappeared. I was waiting weeks between calls from them. I didn't care anymore. It was time to move on. With a new baby at home, I felt pressured to find something with more potential. And as usual, when I'd stopped looking, something leapt from the pages of our local paper. It was a small advertisement, proclaiming it could set you on the path to an exciting career in the world of Hairstyling!

I could do that, I thought. *I've always been interested in doing hair. I have an eye for artsy stuff. I can do that*!

I told Elly about the ad. She figured it was worth a try. I'd been giving her haircuts for years, and that was without knowing the tricks of the trade. So I dialed the number and was greeted at the other end by a guy named Terry. He put me through to the school's owner-operator and we set up an appointment time. The school was right at the end of our street, and perhaps a block or two down Main Street. Not that I'd want to walk back and forth, but I could if I had to.

The day I stepped through the doors of that school, I knew I was making the right choice. Most of the students were girls, of course, but there were a couple guys in there. The Terry I'd spoken to on the phone was an instructor, and a queer. I knew his family from our Elgin Street days. The owner was a pretty-faced heavyset woman, with a bubbly disposition. Her school had been running for about five years already; I had never noticed it. We discussed the terms and conditions of her school, and payment. I was terrified, but I really wanted to do this.

Before my next meeting with the owner, which was to sign a

contract and pay a first installment of my tuition, Elly and I had decided that she, too, should take the course. We could eventually open our own salon and be self-employed—together. It sounded like a solid plan to me. Paying for our tuition put us through one of our poorest years ever. The owner was thrilled to have us, have her first married couple in the school. We gave her a pile of post-dated checks and somehow managed to pay her in monthly install-ments. It worked to our advantage because there were no debts to follow.

We enlisted Mom to baby-sit Chanel for us for the entire ten month course. Since we were still on assistance, Mom was paid for her time. The start of the course was difficult for Elly, leaving Chanel all day. She was still breastfeeding. At lunch hour, she would race home to feed the baby, then race back. Mom started Chanel on bottle feedings, which Chanel refused to accept in the beginning, but soon gave in and let Elly off the hook.

We quickly learned about salon drama. Terry, the instructor, was dealing with a group of immature girls, fresh out of high school. The arguing that went on amongst the girls was annoying and disruptive. An important aspect of the school was its pedestrian clientele. Women and men alike came in off the street for hair cuts, colors, perms, and highlights. And the girls would bicker at one another in front of the clients. It was so unprofessional.

The situation between Terry and a couple students intensified. Those students were kicked out of the school and Terry ended up being let go. We were relieved. We weren't paying all that money to put up with bullshit from these teenyboppers. Some of the girls were pretty snotty in there, especially the few who were ready to graduate. But once they moved on, the student body settled down to a much quieter bunch. And replacing Terry was a hairstylist who would go from being at odds with me to becoming a good friend and mentor.

Anne lived in an apartment right across the street from the school. Elly and I both mistook her for being older than we were, when she was quite a few years younger. The extra weight she car-ried in those days made all the difference. As time went on, the owner never seemed to be there, leaving her new instructor to run the school in her absence. We all took advantage of this, having a far more enjoyable experience than we would have been allowed. I even brought my video camera a few times.

I wasn't the only male student, either. A short kid with blond hair and a smartass attitude was dragging his way through the course. He was a fairly good hairstylist, but his academic marks were far below average. It wasn't that he didn't understand his studies, but the kid could barely read. At his age it didn't make sense. He'd started months before Elly and I, but we would end up graduating before him on account of his poor reading skills. I never knew if he liked me or not. I don't think he did because I was competition in the hair department. And I was progressing beyond him.

Though he never announced his sexuality to the school, we all knew he was queer. I knew he was. My problem was that *I* wasn't supposed to be. I was a married man with children. I just happen to like hairstyling. And I just happen to find myself sneaking a peek at that kid's hairy legs whenever he wore shorts. I wondered if he'd ever caught my glances. They were never at him; I didn't find him attractive at all. He actually annoyed the hell out of me, but I checked out his nice legs, nonetheless. I was so accustomed to my sexual thoughts about men that it didn't really bother me that I snuck peeks (I'd been sneaking peeks my whole life).

As the months passed, I was beginning to tire of the school. I was sick of the routine. Same clients—same fucking roller sets. One lady I was doing a roller set on mentioned the name of one of the other students. "What ever happened to so-and-so?" she asked me. "She was so nice. Did she quit working here?"

I guffawed. "Quit?" I said. "She didn't quit, she graduated! Didn't you know this was a school?"

Yeah, half of those older women had no idea they were our Ginny pigs. I remember feeling nervous about the inevitable graduation day, and finding a job somewhere. I was petrified that I wouldn't know enough, wouldn't be confident enough to work anywhere. Maybe I needed longer than ten months. How could that be sufficient learning time? I was scared to death of landing that first job. But somewhere during the fifth or sixth month of training, I lost all fears. Fellow students were coming to me for help. I was Anne's backup. I understood how the cuts were supposed to work, and had a knack for copying styles out of magazines.

I looked forward to school every day. Elly and I were flying through our tests with ease. The owner often confided in me that I had enormous potential; however, both she and Anne would whisper their doubts about Elly's long term success to me. I knew they were right, but I stuck up for her, claiming that experience would do well by her. Comparing her to me was unfair. We were husband and wife, not identical twins!

Elly and I graduated on the same day, a day that seemed to refuse to end: the ninth day of April 2001. Once we walked out of that school, I felt good, but I also felt a little sad about it. One of my elderly clients cried as she hugged me goodbye. She was sweet. But another client, Jim R., would follow me from the school and become my longest standing client, and a much appreciated friend.

Not By Choice

The one salon we'd heard nothing but rotten things about would, of course, be the one to call us. From their very first contact, this company, which I shall keep nameless, gave us the runaround. We had applied at a location near to us, yet they were offering positions in Niagara Falls. They said they currently had no openings in Welland. We turned them down. One day later, they called again, this time with an opening for just one of us. I expressed my disappointment with this, and I swear, not two minutes later, they phoned a third time and apologized, saying they were unaware that their Welland store was in dire need of BOTH of us. Yes, and so we were hired.

We split our shifts and each worked part time, sharing equal hours at work and at home with the kids. The salon bullshit took about a minute to start. Our store manager was thee biggest pain in my ass I ever had the displeasure of knowing. At 22-years-old, Donna was an immature brat. She acted as if she was the salon's owner, taking great pleasure in bossing her elders around. She rubbed everyone the wrong way. She nitpicked on everything from the shoes I was wearing to the color my eyes were. I always knew when her beady eyes were stabbing at the back of my head.

Donna had no respect for her coworkers or the clients. Many times she came up beside me and demanded to know if the client was, "Paying for that style?" See, if you blow-dried anyone's hair into anything that appeared to have style, she wanted them charged for it. But she was dealing with me, and I'm a stubborn bastard. I began to talk to the other employees about Donna's horrendous behavior. Turned out I was not the only one she was pissing off.

For months we put up with Donna's mismanagement of the salon. We even got together and wrote a grievance about her to the company owners. Signed by all but one of the eight staff members, our letter pretty much went unnoticed. They gave Donna a chance to respond to our complaints, which she did, which I read, and it spelled liar. It seemed as though we'd be stuck with her forever. That was until I became ill with tonsillitis. Donna was harassing Elly every day that I was away, demanding a doctor's note from me. By the third day, I contacted the area manager and *I* demanded that she put an end to Donna's badgering.

"I'm a man," I said, angrily. "I've had many jobs, and never have I had to put up with this kind of harassment. Why would Elly bring in my doctor's note anyway. I'll bring the damn note in when I return to work. I haven't even gone to the doctor's yet," I said, barely able to raise my voice above the level of pain I was experiencing.

The area manager apologized profusely, telling me not to worry about a note, and guaranteeing me that she would take care of Donna. We ended our call at that point. I remember trembling with anger. Within a few moments, the area manager phoned me back and said, "Don't worry about Donna, she just quit."

Man, that was enough to make my suffering worth every aching swallow, and then some! The happier atmosphere in the salon was even noticed by clients. We all wore smiles. My clientele increased by great numbers after that. Soon the seating area would be full of people waiting their turn in my chair. The other girls didn't mind, they could sit on their asses and get paid for doing nothing but watch me work. I certainly didn't mind. The hours passed quickly for me. I loved my work again. Even the head honchos took notice in their store's profit increase. Too bad they weren't smart enough to reward us for it.

Our next manager was another coworker. She was reluctant to take the position, but we all convinced her to. Things ran smoothly for a while, but I don't know, I think the title of manager automatically goes to people's heads and they turn ignorant. It's like a manager's sickness or something (wear the honor—wear the attitude). That poor girl tried her best to keep her head about her. But in the end, she collapsed under pressure, quit, and moved on to another salon.

Now there were five of us, five of the original employees. Our next manager was also reluctant to take on the position. But with my coaxing, and my offer to help with the managerial duties, she accepted. The company gave me a small pay increase for the extra work I was doing. The experience, I thought, could only benefit me. I know I could have done a better job managing, but I didn't want to deal with the extra meetings. The girls all came to me with their complaints, as if I was really in a position to implement any meaningful changes.

We must have seen more than a dozen different stylists come and go. One such stylist, who had two very young sons at home, joined our staff with a shady history. I knew nothing about her, nor do I suspect the other girls did either, but that didn't stop them from treating her with indignity. Even Elly didn't seem to like her. I ended up working a closing shift with her one night. The salon was dead so we were able to get to know each other. And from that night forward, we were friends. I saw a change in the other girls once they noticed the relaxed working relationship between us.

It was about that time that I received a call from the owner of our hairstyling school. She offered me a job as an instructor at her school. My heart fluttered. I would have loved to teach. "I know you would. I saw that in you," she said.

But her wages were much lower than what I was presently earning. There was just no way I could accept. As much as I wanted to work for her, I couldn't.

Anyone Get The License Of The Truck That Hit Me?

Just when things seemed to be on the straight and narrow, something began to happen to me. I wondered if my unrelenting fatigue was due to the extra work I was doing, both for the salon, and with my own clientele at home. I was earning money under the table, doing hair in our basement. I had my own salon set up, with a chair Bev had picked up at a secondhand store, and a sink my aunt had found at a yard sale. Jim was a regular.

The harmony in the salon at work never lasted long. Once again the girls were at each other's throats, and I seemed always caught in the middle. I was their peacekeeper. Even Trudy, whom I had the most fun with, was suddenly getting on my nerves. She was so predictable in every way: her hairstyles, her jokes, her complaints, and her mistakes. Even the way she spoke up on my behalf (something I'd never asked her to do) when anyone questioned my sexuality. She was quick to inform them I was married with children. I hated that. As if it mattered who I was fucking. I was the best stylist in there.

I had my share of run-ins with nasty people, and guess what, they were all seniors. One old lady looked me up and down when I called her name. "*You're* gonna cut my hair? A *man*? I've never had *a man* cut my hair," she said, shaking her head.

I remember Trudy backing me up once again, saying, "Yep. He's the best, Mrs. Mikey's your man."

That didn't persuade the old bat. Having had her type before, I just walked away, pretending I was indifferent to her ignorance. She wasn't the first such person, nor was she the last. In fact, it seemed as though someone had unlocked the doors at the old folks home and purposely set them on me in droves. That same week another senior came slinking in. One of the girls was sitting behind the reception desk, but it was my turn to do the next cut. I came forward from the back room, wearing a plaid shirt and my scissor belt, smiling.

"Can I get your name, Sir," asked the girl.

The old man didn't even glance at her; he was too busy glaring at me. I didn't even get the chance to greet him. He looked me in the eyes, and in a raspy arrogant tone, he asked, "What are you supposed to be…the plumber?"

I looked down at the other girl, still smiling, and said, "Ah. I'm not doing him."

Whoever she was, she laughed along with me as I turned and walked away.

I'd learned not to let miserable clients bring me down, but that week was different. It wasn't just the satanic seniors, or Trudy's over zealous defending of my dignity, or the constant bickering of the other girls, or my personal dealings with our manager's lack of competence; it was all of the above. I was tired—exhausted. My subtle trembling condition (Essential Tremor) was interfering with my cutting ability. I was working with a headache every shift, and every shift the manager would come into the back room, where I'd be rubbing my eyes, and ask me what was wrong. I finally exploded on her and reminded her that I'd explained about the headaches a dozen times already, and to stop asking.

Finally, during one shift with Trudy, I felt this sudden thrust of pain in my chest. I knew well enough that it wasn't my usual murmur. I finished my cut and headed to the washroom to throw water on my face. Trudy left her customer to check on me; she'd noticed the ghostly white wash over my face. I assured her I was fine, but I wasn't. The headache I'd forced under control with drugs was back with a vengeance. I couldn't get out of there quick enough. When I got home, I told Elly about the symptoms I'd been dealing with. She was going for a doctor's appointment the very next day, to *our* doctor. I gave her an explicit list of symptoms to pass on to him. I asked her to tell him that I thought I might be having a nervous breakdown, and wanted to know if he thought I should just ignore it or come in to see him. Of course, he said to come in right away.

The following day I paid a visit to our doctor. He was one year younger than I was, and without a doubt, the friendliest man I'd ever known. We didn't know each other too well at that point, but that would all change, drastically. He and I were on a first name only basis right from our first meeting, so I called him Liam. When Liam entered the office that afternoon, I don't think he was expecting to find me in the condition I was in. Nor had I realized, until that meeting, how far gone I was.

Liam shook my hand and sat behind his desk. He always looked so relaxed at work. I was sitting in a chair opposite to him. He was happy to see me, but he wasted no time in getting me to describe to him just what it was that convinced me I was experiencing a breakdown. "So, Mike, what's going on? Tell me what symptoms you're having."

"You really want to know all of them?" I asked, trying to kid a little. Then I began: "Well, my tremors are really bad. I have to hold my cutting hand with my free hand just to keep it steady. I can't concentrate. I keep forgetting what I was saying in mid sentence. I have these headaches every day, all day, from morning till night. They just won't go away. Everything's driving me nuts. I can't take the people at work any more. I'm so tired all the time. I can't sleep, and when I finally fall asleep all I do is dream. And yesterday I had pain in my chest that nearly made me sick and..."

And as I was rambling on, Liam was leaning over his desk, closer and closer to me. His eyes were wide as if he was in a state of amazement. He finally interrupted me.

"*Mike*, look at you! You're a mess, buddy. You have to take care of this right now," he said, with urgency in his tone.

And he was right. When I stopped talking, I realized I'd been rubbing my head and wriggling like I had ants in my pants. I was beyond self-repair. I was beyond ignoring this thing I'd become—a wreck. I was in need of a major tune-up, and some major drugs. I wasn't exhausted and frustrated for nothing. I...was...sick!

"I'm taking you off work," said Liam, writing a note. "You

have to take care of this. You're at risk for a stroke or heart-attack. You're taking time off work. Those assholes, making you sick like this. You deserve better. You're better than that place, Mikey."

Funny, a million people could tell me how good I was at something, but when Liam said it, I believed it. I followed his instructions as far as the drug he'd prescribed. Elly handed my sick note in at work. Everyone was shocked, except the manager, she just didn't get it—ever. And then it really hit me: I succumbed to my sickness.

Racked With Pain

I'm so tired—three words that had made their home on my tongue. My voice was lost to me, my neck was stiff, and my ears were plugged. I had one headache; just one headache that would never let up. I was weaker now. The nerve under my left eye wouldn't stop jittering. My entire being was crashing. Liam prescribed an antidepressant called Paxil C.R. He'd started me on 10 milligrams. Meanwhile, Elly took over my shifts at work since I was given three weeks off. I don't remember ever hearing her complain. She didn't really comment on my ailment, either. I would tell her about...oh...wait... That's why she didn't comment, I think. I was nagging so much about my sufferings, she'd probably learned to block me out.

I'd reached the breaking point. My body was racked with pain. Intense muscle cramps filled me with agonizing torment. Every inch of my skin seemed to scream out for attention. Using a bathtub sauna Tammy had given me, my new bed was filled with hot water and bubbles. There was no escaping the pain. Once I came out of the tub, I felt so weak it was all I could do to walk from the washroom to our bedroom, where I'd collapse on the bed. The slightest bit of relief I'd gained from the baths would diminish within the hour. I would lie in bed squirming, unable to relax myself out of my aching. So I'd return to the bath for another soak; it was all I could do, and all I did for weeks on end.

Clearly, the medication wasn't helping me. Liam increased the dosage to 15 milligrams. It didn't make a difference. I felt as if my brain was flooded and my thoughts were drowning. I couldn't do anything or go anywhere. My farthest journey was from the bedroom to the living room, where I'd sleep on the sofa for hours at a time. I was missing the kids, but I couldn't bear the sounds of their voices, even when they weren't yelling. I remember having to leave the dinner table one night because their talking caused me to tense up and tremble uncontrollably. I was in hell.

Weeks were turning into months, and still I wasn't showing signs of recovering. Liam had increased my dosage once again, up to 20 milligrams now. Word from work was that there was no word; my coworkers couldn't care less about my health. Trudy was the only one who'd ask about me. My clients were beginning to worry, though. Some even thought I'd quit. A family consisting of two sisters and their mother sent me a huge gift basket. Needless to say, they are still my clients today.

It was Thursday, June 10 2004, when Mom and Tammy dropped in to check on me. I was lying on the sofa feeling sleepy—dizzy—and unable to stop writhing due to my restless limbs. Mom and Tammy took to cleaning the house for us. They went on a rampage cleaning upstairs, downstairs, in the kitchen, and even helping out with the laundry. I didn't care what they were doing, it just felt good to know someone was in the house with me. It brought a much needed comfort to me, knowing I wasn't alone. And I knew Mom understood what I was experiencing; she'd suffered three breakdowns herself in the past.

By my next visit with Liam, I'd broken out in hives. I told him about my violent nightmares. I'd been physically reacting to my dreams, kicking Elly, punching, and screaming out. Sleeping in the same bed with me was risky business. I'd even kicked our poor little pup off the bed. My absence from work was about to last longer. Liam had no choice but to increase my dosage from 20 mgs to 25 mgs. As he scribbled the new prescription down, he warned me, saying, "Now, Mike, you're probably gonna hate my guts for this. There's gonna be side effects."

"Oh, great. Just what I need—side effects," I said sarcastically.

Liam slid the note across his desk toward me, staring into my eyes as if to be sure I was listening and understanding.

"No. Really, Mike. Everyone reacts to this drug differently. There are a dozen side effects you might experience but you have to be strong and get past them. Whatever you do, don't quit the drug. Okay?"

"I won't," I said.

"Don't quit," Liam stressed.

When I left his office that day, I wondered how critical the side effects were going to be. Just what was I about to get myself into? I'll never forget, when I got home Chanel immediately started to rash me for some photograph she wanted. I told her she'd have to wait, that I didn't know where it was, and I would have to dig it out. And she asked, "Why? Is it in the dirt?"

She could really come out with some head-turners; but Hunter, now he was the crowning king of quirky comments. One night, after having been up in his bed for about half an hour, he came back down stairs.

"Hunter," I called to him, "what's wrong?"

Rubbing his eyes, he said, "My bed was making me sleepy."

While Hunter's bed might have been the culprit behind *his* sleepiness, my new and improved dosage of Paxil was doing its best to keep me under sedation. I began to yawn uncontrollably as well; the yawns were coming about every three to four minutes apart—and they felt so good. At least the muscle aches had subsided. I was much happier having to deal with yawns and drowsiness than pain and nightmares. It became apparent that I was over the worst of the sickness—finally—and I'd only missed FOUR MONTHS of work.

The Blue Man

My recovery was a long and slow process. In fact, I would never wake up and feel quite like the man I was prior to the breakdown. I might as well have been crippled in an accident because the wounds inflicted within me were not going to be magically expelled by medicines or faith. This was now something I would have to learn to live with and manage the best I could, with a continued daily use of Paxil as a helping hand. The headaches would persist, the dizziness, and the tremors; but there was no denying the healing had begun.

By late August, against Liam's advice, I insisted he allow me to return to work. Said I needed to be out of the house again, and back in the swing of life. So I returned, starting at only two days a week. I was ecstatic to be going back to that shithole. The girls welcomed me with hugs, especially Trudy. The manager was another story. She said two words to me through the entire day: Hi... and Bye. As I worked, I felt like my limbs were wrapped in concrete. But I didn't care. I needed the atmosphere.

I had five requests that day, and I was sure to slip them my personal business card, with my home phone number on it. Clients were happy to see me, and more than happy to accept my cards. They were eager to fill me in on the disrespect I'd received behind my back from my coworkers. Even worse—they had to endure lousy haircuts in my absence. Many of them were led to believe I would not be returning. I knew this was going to be the final stretch at this job for me. I had to enlist as many of my clients as I could to follow me into the next stage of my career—self-employment!

My return to work came just in time to reunite with Trudy during her final week as an employee with us. She'd taken all she could of the company and was moving on. It was tough enough working in our salon, but without Trudy? I adored her, but I didn't feel the way I thought I would about her leaving. I was preparing my own exit from the salon. One way or another, Trudy and I were going to be separated. I was glad she wasn't being left behind. I knew this to be her own fears as well, having had conversations about our quitting on several occasions. We would meet again.

Someone else I would meet again, after a six year interval, which neither one of us could excuse, was Dwayne. He must have tuned in on my blues. It did me a world of good to see him, and a world of grief to watch him go. I learned how instant my sickness switch could be turned on. My head was swirling and my level of energy dipped down into my toes. My blood brother's visit had drained every dollar of strength I had and left me penniless. Six years had been too long.

Then, another friend would unwittingly drag my spirits down. It was easy—I wasn't well enough to withstand the slightest negative emotions. This time, something as petty as a house-call for a haircut would be the antagonist. Feeling as though I owed so much to my doctor friend, Liam, I offered him my services for free. He was always telling me how great a stylist I was, and how much better than the company I worked for I was, and yet he had never experienced my skills. So I offered, and he accepted, and we had set the day and...he didn't show.

I tried to be adult about it. Tried not to take it personally, or to heart, or in any way as a comment on our friendship. I tried. But if blue is the color of depression, then I was a blue man. Liam had given me a prescription for muscle-relaxers to ease my headaches and help me sleep (too bad I couldn't afford to have the prescription filled). I didn't have the balls to tell him and expose myself as the pathetic loser I was. So the muscle spasms and sleepless nights became the norm.

PART 2

Dream House

It was March 2005, Elly and I had finally quit that shithole salon. The owner knew damn well that he was losing his best stylists, so he made an offer through our manager. She said he couldn't afford to lose us and wanted to know what he could possibly do to change our minds. Of course, there was nothing he could do to change *my* mind, which was made up long before my resignation was announced. For the hell of it, we told the manager we wanted a raise and a set schedule; no more of this never knowing what shifts you were going to be working. I'd just tossed it out there; I really had no intention to stay. Three days after our response, the assholes said they couldn't comply.

So, why bother asking what we wanted? I wondered.

Meanwhile, Trudy telephoned us from her new job. She described a work environment from heaven, with better pay, less employees, a wonderful manager, and an all around finer salon. She told us the manager was really interested in hiring us on. Within about a week's time, we were employed with Trudy again. Elly was working full time, but I continued with only two days per week (it was all I could handle, yet). Basically, Trudy had been correct in her descriptions of the place, with a couple minor exaggerations.

My first impression of this new salon was that it was much cleaner and self-sufficient. It was equipped with two standing tanning booths and a computer register. The tanning booths were no bother, but the register was a mind-boggling electric puzzle to me. Just to punch in a freaking haircut, you had to run through an entire system of crap. Whatever happened to the good old cash registers?

Who gives a shit if my name is on the receipt?

Anyway, the register was just one annoyance. Aside from Trudy, there were only two other employees: the manager and a young, unlicensed girl. The young girl was knocked up, so I knew she wouldn't be around long. Good thing, too. I'd watched her in action and it stressed me out. She had no skill whatsoever. And the manager, well, I think she tried too hard to be hip. She thought that riding to work on her Harley automatically made her "cool." But her foul mouth, which was constant, and uncensored in front of little children, revealed the fool she truly was.

I was doing fairly well for myself back home. My clientele had tripled in numbers; I was able to put money aside for our future. That was the first time in my life I could save. So the few days I worked at the salon weren't making much of a difference in my pocket. For that reason, when I worked my last shift on a Sunday afternoon with Trudy, I was confident my quitting was the best move for me, and for my health.

In all the years I'd worked alongside Trudy, I was only just aware of her lack of aptitude. She was able to hide her butcher jobs within her styles, until clients returned a couple days later, complaining about their inability to manage the mess. So, yeah, I knew she wasn't the greatest. Her personality got her by. I never understood how she could cut hair with those long nails of hers. Wow, what a character she was. She'd put on these false eyelashes individually—camel lashes, I called them. Her hair was bleached white and styled funky. She wore about five or six dangling earrings in each ear, earrings so heavy that the pierced holes were stretched open. On the heftier side, she pretty much looked like the witch from Disney's *The Little Mermaid.*

It was during our last Sunday working together that I was able to sit and watch the gal at work. Keep in mind that it still didn't take much of anything to cause my stress to flare up into physical reactions. The salon was slow, as it was every hour of every day. Not a busy location, I guess is what I'm saying. We took turns attending to the customers. I'd cut, she'd cut, I'd cut, she'd cut... There was never more than one customer in there at a time.

Trudy was quite the gabber. Unfortunately, she was gabbing to me and not to the customers she was working on. I was sitting at my station, directly behind hers. She had to turn completely around to face me, which she kept doing as she talked. I could see how one man's frustration with her was mushrooming. But far worse than her gabbing was the fact that her cutting was unbelievably horrendous. There was no knowledge behind her technique: she just hacked away!

Snip here. Snip there. Should have snipped *there*, but didn't. Her perimeters were about as straight as...well, as I am! I had to witness horror after horror. I couldn't take it. I'm not claiming to be an expert at cutting hair, but what she got away with—Chanel could do better—blindfolded and strung up by her heels! And that's all it took to end my days working for someone else. When I got home that evening, I was exhausted. The stress of my shift left my hands trembling, my neck stiff, and my head swooning. I spared no anger when I explained to Elly about Trudy, and how I'd made up my mind to quit.

"I make enough money on my own. I don't need their weekends," I said. "I'm finished!"

Elly didn't say much. She couldn't understand what I was ranting on about anyway. Or she didn't care. I'd been talking about working for myself for a while. She was probably tired of hearing it. When I slipped into bed that night, I remember feeling a great peace befall me. No more computer register, no more managers, no more sitting around between clients, and no more bearing witness to bad haircuts. I was done with that. I was done with it all.

A few days later, we had a mortgage manager come to our house. Neither Elly nor myself thought for one second that we would qualify to buy a house...but we did! Turns out, all we needed was to find a willing co-signer. Elly's mother, unaware of what co-signing truly meant, readily agreed to be ours. It appeared that things were looking up for us.

Within weeks, Elly and I had signed our names a dozen or so times on dotted lines. I don't know about her, but I only vaguely understood the mumbo-jumbo in those contracts. *Yeah, yeah, I get it—pay money to live in house.* We'd secured the very house our dreams were made of. It had everything we wanted: wood floors, wood kitchen cabinets, a fireplace, an attic with potential to remodel, three bedrooms, a wreck room, a basement we could finish into a family room, and fancy molding around the living room and dining room ceilings.

We knew instantly that this was *our* house, *our* dream house. And by August of 2005, we were settling in. Mr. East helped solve electrical and plumbing problems we had in setting our salon up in the living room. We purchased two new salon chairs, a couple trolley trays, a desk for the register we thought we needed, and a few other necessities. We then repainted every room and gave it our personal touches. With everything finding its place, we were home at last.

The Swing of Things

I continued in our new house right where I'd left off in our old one: taking clients at home. Elly was still holding her job with Trudy. I think she feared the idea of being self-employed. There was no guaranteed check at the end of every two weeks. She had not steered her work clients in our direction, either. So as my clientele continued to grow, Elly's remained the same. A couple months past before she gave her notice to quit. But once she did, we began to feel like a team.

The house was no palace but we were content. Every day we'd sit in the far corner of the backyard, under the shade of a Maple tree, and drink our coffees. It was like living a commercial moment from TV. One of my cousins, who we'd worked on and off with, had opened her own salon just down the street from us. Her salon space was much too great for what she needed, and she had to rent a chair to another girl to cover costs. She was doing well enough.

Our first summer in our new house was exciting. For once, all the painting and decorating we did was truly for us. There were no flowers planted around the property, so we went from Mom's to Bev's, to Tammy's, to Elly's mother's, and Elly's sister's, gathering up as many different types of plants as we were allowed. The greatest amount and variety came from Bev's backyard. Hers was a garden paradise. Our yard had plenty of spaces for planting, and I did my best to fill them all in. Though there was much work to be done, we were loving it.

That same month, Tammy was hired on to drive the city Transit. She'd been trying to get that job for a couple years, and then, just like that, it was hers. Debbie was about to move into her new Welland home from Beamsville, where she'd been lonely for six or seven years. Bev's daughter was pregnant for the second time, expecting a son as it were. And Chanel was facing all-day schooling in the up and coming year. Changes in our family were plentiful.

Not all changes to come would be good ones, however. By December, Tate and Mona had split up. Seems Tate had done the nasty with an old tenant of theirs. I knew renting out the upper apartment of their house was going to mean trouble. A phone call I'd made to Dwayne on his thirty-sixth birthday revealed more bad news: he and *his* wife had also split up, sharing custody of their 5-year-old son, Wyatt. Soon we'd have a visitor with more bad news.

In the meantime, however, my relationship with Liam was bringing me closer to him. He'd become like a brother to me. Not since meeting Dwayne had I felt so in sync with someone. He told Mom I was his best friend. I know I could never quit him as a doctor, simply because I'd miss him. Unfortunately, between work and family, Liam had no time for me outside the office. My cousin's husband, who was eight years younger than I, had become a pretty good friend, though. He was one of those people you meet and instantly form a bond with.

He and my cousin had made some shitty life choices in the past couple years. I tried to warn them, but my cousin, once she'd made up her mind, would not listen to reason. She'd convinced Lee to quit his job and move to her sister's house in Fenwick, where he was to secure another job before sending for her and their three kids. So he did. He went out there and got a job. About three months later, my cousin gave up their apartment to join him—still at her sister's. It didn't work, and after losing all they'd had here in Welland, they came back to nothing.

They landed at her parent's house and had to begin again. I was glad. Not because I'd been right about the move being wrong, but because I had my friends back. Soon after, they bought a small house with her parent's help, and gave up their Fenwick dreams forever. Lee took a course and became a Personal Support Worker—a nurse—or as I liked to tease him—a wiper of old people's butts! My cousin returned to work as a hairstylist, until she and Lee rented her own salon, as I'd mentioned.

So, now that I brought you back full circle on my account of their lives, I can tell you why. Things were good for Elly and I. We were a legalized business in our hometown, and feeling like we'd finally accomplished something for ourselves. We were at the end of May, just past Randee and Taylor's twelfth birthdays and Hunter's eleventh. And on one of those warm beautiful days, Lee stopped in for a visit. He'd made a habit of dropping by for a coffee break. I liked his company. I saw him quite a bit more than I saw my cousin, his wife.

I was busy cleaning up after a customer as he sat at our dining room table. Elly was doing something as well. All I remember is looking at my friend's face and thinking to myself, *Something's not right with him.*

"Well," he started, "since you're going to find out anyway, I might as well be the one to tell you."

Lee hid his face in his hands as he wept. He told us he and my cousin were splitting up. Since the night of her thirtieth birthday, she'd decided a change in life was what she needed. She no longer thought of him sexually, or even as her husband! He was told she felt like he was just another relative. She'd urged him to seek out another girlfriend, and start his own *new* life. As far as she was concerned, their thirteen years of marriage was finished.

With nowhere to go, Elly and I did not hesitate to open our house to him. In a matter of a week or two, Lee was living with us. I thought it was great. It was like having a brother to hang with again. Diagnosed with type one Diabetes at age fifteen, Lee's sugars had been out-of-whack for some time. But after being with Elly and me, his sugars began to regulate, and his outlook wasn't so grim. He'd moved in just in time to celebrate Elly's thirty-ninth birthday. Well, okay, we really didn't celebrate, but it was her birthday.

I'd been for another visit to see Liam. He'd made a promise to come to me for a haircut—again—but again he didn't show for it. I wanted so much for him to see our salon and see me in the swing of things. I don't know, I guess it was stupid. I don't know why it meant so much to me.

Following the disappointment of being stood up by Liam, the weekend turned out to be wonderful. Dwayne came down and spent the night with Wyatt and his new girlfriend. Chris was a breath of new life; she was everything Dwayne needed in a partner. Wyatt appeared perfectly comfortable with her. She was far better-looking than the ex, and a lot more fun. I think I detected a bit of jealousy from Dwayne because of Lee's presence. He made a few comments about Lee, which I brushed off. By the time Dwayne, Chris, and Wyatt pulled out of our driveway (Dwayne singing along with a country song) I was exhausted. Trying to keep up with Dwayne's limitless energy is impossible. No wonder kids love him so.

The minute I'd stepped foot back into the house, the sadness I'd been feeling lately wrapped its invisible hands around my throat and squeezed. It wasn't the usual (Dwayne is gone) sadness, either. This was different. I'd been feeling down for a while. It was the weight of this incredible secret I'd been keeping since I was a kid. After all those years, I was still guarding it with my life. My only means of maintaining some speck of sanity was to allow myself to leak once in a while. So, as if I'd slit my wrist, and felt the sweet warm liquid ooze from my body, through poetry I found subtle release.

Secret

A flame blazes within me. The door is barred. And I am full of fever.
It's all life. It's me, of me, from me, because of me.
It eats me and feeds me. I breathe it and bathe in it.
It's keeping me alive—it's *killing* me!
As the flame burns I peel.
I have fears crawling around in my mouth, and I cannot speak a word of what they are.
So I kneel here, naked and parched.
I know what the beads of perspiration are craving as they slice down my skin, laughing and screaming.
I've ached to hush them, but I cannot.

My true self remains imprisoned in shackles of immiscible lives.
So closeted is my affliction, I may never arrive.

A Doctor Without A Stethoscope Is Just Another Man

I WAS BEGINNING TO THINK I would need a second doctor to deal with my problems with Liam. Or, perhaps, he needed a doctor. On a Friday, he actually stopped by. He knew I needed to talk to him. Upon his arrival, I greeted him in our backyard. He appeared to be very uncomfortable and shy. I had just sat down with him when another client showed up, and I had to step inside. Liam said he'd wait, but when I went back out, he was gone.

Then he phoned me from his car to explain that he was going to a show with his wife or something. He set a time to come back that Sunday (and did he?) Of course not. No Liam and no phone call. I was so depressed. *Maybe*, I thought, *he couldn't get passed the Doctor-Patient relationship.* I didn't know. I was getting mixed signals from him. Maybe he was just so good at his job that I was being fooled into believing in a connection that wasn't really there. I just didn't know.

A couple weeks later, I rode a bicycle to his office, determined to set the record straight, at least in my mind. It was just the two of us, chatting. There were some awkward moments, but in general, he seemed to understand what I was trying (sloppily) to get across. It wouldn't be the end of my disappointments with him, nor my confusion; the trek across the glass-covered floor was only beginning. It would soon become clear to me that the shards were spreading into every part of my life.

One afternoon, Elly and I were sitting in the salon with the girls, looking through photo albums. Lee was upstairs in his room exercising, or so we thought. We'd heard a loud thump and assumed he'd dropped one of the dumbbells. A few minutes after, I decided I'd better go up and check on him. When I tried to open the door to his room, I found it was blocked by something, and that something was Lee!

I squeezed my way into the room, calling out Lee's name. He was lying in a heap unconscious, behind the door. I tried to revive him without success. Calling down to Elly to telephone for an ambulance, I lugged Lee's body off the floor and flopped him face-down on the bed. He was starting to come around, but immediately began to cry out about the excruciating pain in his head. I ran for a washcloth and returned to rub the back of his head, neck, and shoulders with it.

Elly hadn't made the call yet. She came up to see what was happening. I yelled at her to call the ambulance. Chanel was standing in the doorway, meanwhile, watching Lee squirm in pain. I told her to go to her room. Just when it seemed like the pain in Lee's head was never going to subside…he breathed a breath of relief. Of course, that's about when the two ambulance guys came in. I explained what had occurred as I stepped aside, allowing them to question Lee and perform simple tests on him.

With a medic under each arm, Lee fumbled his way downstairs. I followed them out to the ambulance and rode to the hospital with them. It was my first time in an ambulance, and I was glad to be a passenger and not a patient. Once we arrived at the hospital, we lied and said I was Lee's brother (to me it wasn't so much a lie as a slight exaggeration). I remained there with him for most of the day. Even got to meet the doctor whose head was surrounded by flies. He kept waving them away, but he definitely smelled like something they liked.

Whatever had caused Lee's seizure seemed to have dispersed. After three hot days in the damned hospital, eating their TV Dinners, Lee was released, none the wiser than when he'd arrived there. For all their specialized tests, the doctors could not find the cause of his collapse. I urged Lee to pursue the matter beyond our local quacks, and consult with a specialist before another attack. I don't think he did.

Chanel handed him a little note upon his return home. It was so cute. Misspelled words expressed her love and worry for him.

She'd demonstrated a great deal more humanity than Lee's wife had. She knew he was in the hospital, but she never once brought their children to see him. His own family didn't bother to visit him there. It was shameful. But while he was having his troubles, I was about to trade my carpet of broken glass for a bed of nails.

Pilate To Bombardier: Bombs Away!

I cannot recall when the visits began: under my nose, behind my back, so casually and innocently; but they began. Hunter was spending much of his free time going to a local Serpentarium (reptile zoo). The owner/operator was an Australian fellow, who was teaching Hunter everything he needed to know about reptiles. I thought the amount of knowledge Hunter had obtained was admirable. You could show him the photo of any snake and he could tell you its name and characteristics.

He was allowed to hold the snakes and feed them, learning all about proper handling techniques. What started out as a boy's curiosity became an obsession. Elly drove Hunter to the Serpentarium every night at six o'clock, then returned to pick him up at nine o'clock. I didn't think there was anything shady going on, until Elly's routine changed. Instead of just dropping our son off, she was now staying there with him, coming home later than the usual nine o'clock closing.

I recall the night she and I took the kids to visit at Mona's house. We'd only been there about an hour, when Elly said she was going to pick Hunter up. Mona's house was a mere three streets from the Serpentarium. We thought nothing of it when Elly left, but when she hadn't returned over an hour later, Mona and I both became suspicious. Mona phoned to ask Elly what was taking her so long. She'd made up some excuse. Between Mona and myself, we couldn't understand how Elly could stand to be in a house full of reptiles.

Day after day, Hunter's newly-found hobby seemed to have rubbed off on Elly. Now *she* was rushing him to leave for the Serpentarium, and bringing him home later and later. Eventually, I did ask her what the hell she was doing there. She told me those people were her friends, and it was just a place to hang out. I only half believed her. I wanted to believe her. Why shouldn't I believe her? We were in our sixteenth year of marriage. Why shouldn't I be<u>lie</u>ve her?

As Elly was making 'new friends,' I was struggling with my own feelings. I don't know what it was that made my secret gain strength suddenly, but it wanted to burst out of me like the chest-bursters in the *Alien* movie series. So consumed by my need to share my secret with Elly, I put my doubts about her fidelity aside, ignoring the obvious to cater to my own dilemma. And that was when I met Brian. He'd heard about me from a coworker and set up an appointment to have his hair cut. When I saw him pull up alongside my house, my poor vision momentarily threw me for a spin. Brian not only drove a car similar to the one Liam drove, but he resembled Liam as well.

My first words to Brian were: "Do you have a brother who's a doctor?"

Brian smiled and said, "No."

"Well, you look so much like my doctor, I thought you *were* him at first."

Brian's voice even sounded like Liam's. He was very personable. I took an immediate liking to him. And by about his third or fourth haircut, I'd asked him if it would be okay for he and I to get together for coffee sometime. It wasn't long before he called me up and invited me to a show with him and another friend of his. I was thrilled; I had no friends other than Lee, who'd been spending most of his time with a new girlfriend. Of course I wanted to go.

When Brian picked me up, I felt nervous, like I had a case of stage fright. I didn't want to say anything to jeopardize this new friendship. As we drove along the highway, heading to St.Catharines, Brian handed me a list of the shows he'd printed from the Internet. One of the movies listed was starring hunky Jason Statham. At the mention that I wouldn't mind seeing it, Brian glanced at me and replied, nonchalantly, "The only reason I'd see that movie is to see Jason's body. He's pretty hot."

Seeing the dumbfounded expression on my face, he continued.

"I'm gay. Didn't you know that?"

"No," I said. And then I felt myself sigh tremulously. And my secret, desperate to be free, released itself not as an erupting volcano, but as a whispered confession to a priest.

"I've never told anyone this...but I'm gay too."

As I heard the words roll off my tongue, I didn't feel dirty the way I thought I would. I didn't feel completely bold, either. I just felt terrified.

Brian looked at me and said, "Really? You're saying I'm the first person you've ever told this to?"

I nodded.

"Thank you," he said. "I appreciate that."

We changed the subject, but it never left my mind. Upon meeting Brian's other friend, Pat, their homosexuality was crystal clear to me. Now I saw it in the way Brian walked and talked. How I hadn't seen it before, I couldn't explain. Or had I known all along? What attracted me to Brian in the first place? His friendliness, his appearance, his gayness, or his common attributes to Liam? Now I was truly afraid. What did it all mean? Was I attracted to Liam through brotherly love, or something else? I was shaken. Screw the broken glass and bed of nails, *bombs* were falling all around me and I had nowhere to hide. I made up my mind to do the only thing I could, the same thing I'd always done—ignore it.

Having shared my concerns about Elly with Brian, and knowing how depressed I'd been, he asked me to join him and yet another St.Catharines friend for a night out. The large company they were both employed under was throwing a Halloween dance. But this wasn't just any Halloween dance, it was a dance for all of the company's gay employees. I was hesitant about going, but any time I could spend with Brian, I jumped at.

On the night of the dance, we pulled into Wesly's driveway, behind a van. I followed Brian out to meet his friend, who was saying goodbye to the heavyset woman in the van. I remember just smiling a lot, not knowing anyone, barely knowing Brian. I didn't really take the time to see what this Wesly guy looked like—I was shy. He hopped in the back seat of Brian's car and we drove a ten minute drive to the dance. Mostly everyone was in costume, except the three of us. I would have been better off in a costume, now that I think about it. Funny to admit, too, I'd never gone to an adult Halloween dance, let alone a gay one.

Once we were inside, we each purchased a beer, which I'm not very fond of drinking. Turned out, Wesly was drinking the same brand as I. That opened the door for conversation, and it never closed. He and I were more compatible than I was with Brian. As I watched Brian dance, I remember thinking, *It is true...all gay guys* ***can*** *dance.* He could move but his height and body shape made me giggle to myself about him.

Much to my dismay, in walked a pair of Elly's clients. We'd always known the couple were lesbians, I just wasn't expecting to run into them at the dance.

"What are you doing here?" the prettier one asked me. She was dressed like a police officer and her partner was her prisoner in black and white stripes.

"I'm here with a couple friends," I said, wishing she would just go away and forget she'd seen me.

But it was too late, I'd been seen, and worse than that—I'd been seen dancing a slow dance with Wesly. I couldn't very well lie and say I was there in support of my gay pals. I mean, there's support and then there's dancing a slow dance with another man. I knew Elly's clients would definitely bring it up to her, so I would have to tell her first, keeping my secret under wraps.

I enjoyed the dance, and afterward, we went to the local gay bar and danced some more. It was a night of many firsts for me. Wesly and I danced all night and no one cared. No one pointed fingers. People were watching me, but not for the wrong reasons. Wesly was fun. Can't say I hadn't noticed the rather large-looking lump he was concealing (we do look, you know). By the end of the evening, Brian and I dropped Wesly off. I watched him disappear into the darkness behind his house, where he used the back door to gain entrance. I didn't even get his number, nor did he get mine.

The next day, when describing the Halloween dance to Elly, I led on as if I hadn't known it was a gay dance. I told her about bumping into her clients, the officer and the prisoner. She asked me about Brian.

"Why would he bring you to a gay dance? Does he think *you're* gay? Maybe he likes you," she said in disgust.

"As if," I answered. "He's just a friend."

I changed the subject, confident I had evaded the truth. But was I keeping the truth from Elly, or from myself? Later that day, I joined Brian at his house. He'd just moved into a newly built home a few blocks from me. His elderly parents were sharing the house with him. I followed him into their basement, where he was in the beginning stage of setting up a private space for himself. He was a bit of a computer buff, and a self-reliant electrician as well.

We talked about the dance and Wesly, but I didn't share with him just how much Wesly had remained in my thoughts. Instead, I told him about how I'd lied to Elly. I wasn't comfortable lying to her. I hinted to him that I'd been thinking a lot about coming out to her. He suggested that I think hard about any such plan, weighing the consequences of what I was getting myself into. I knew he was right, but I was foolishly under the impression that Elly would understand. She had to. We'd known each other for so many years. I knew she couldn't possibly doubt my love for her. But this was no regular secret a man shares with his wife. If I'd been having such a hard time accepting who I was, how would she handle it? How indeed?

For our next rendezvous, Brian and I met for coffee at the diner across the street from my house. I had no problem telling him I was harboring a crush on him. He politely told me we could be friends but nothing more. I didn't understand why. I still don't understand why. He once described his perfect man and it sounded a lot like he was describing me. Perhaps my having kids and still being married put me off his list. Whatever his reasons, we never did get 'together.'

Once again, I described to him the inner tug-of-war I was living with, trying to decide whether or not I should share my secret with Elly. The plane of thinking I was on was one which placed great confidence and trust in my wife of sixteen years, and then some. I came to this conclusion: since my love was so great and true for her, hers must be the same for me. So, with that ill-conceived notion, I decided to reveal the last piece of my soul to her (or was it the first piece?)

On a cool but sunny afternoon in late October, while the children were at school, I'd convinced Elly to take a drive with me to our city park, Merritt Island. Having told her that there was something important we needed to discuss, she agreed to go. We parked the car and walked together down to a picnic table, close to the muddy river. Under the flickering shade of a willow tree, I sat on the table-top as Elly stood, sipping from her cardboard coffee cup. She was in a good mood, which made the sick feeling in my stomach all the worse.

I made several false starts to tell her my secret. And now, I could see I was making her uncomfortable. I looked around at the trees and sky, the brown water, Elly's expectant expression; the day seemed perfect (to start a war). It had to be said properly, with care, with clarity. I was trying to get the lines clear in my mind, trying to focus on what I was going to say, and how I was going to say it. I thought I was ready for this moment, yet, there it was, sitting in my lap, waiting on the tip of my tongue, and I was on the verge of freezing up.

Elly was egging me on, sipping her coffee impatiently now. I remember taking a deep breath, which made a chill run through my body. Looking into her eyes, the sun at the corners of mine, I started:

"The things I'm going to tell you, I'm not saying because I want a change in our marriage..."

Her smile slowly became a frown.

"This is something that's been a part of me since I was a kid. I have memories of it that go as far back as I can remember. This doesn't change how I feel about you. I want us to grow old together. But..." I sighed, "...I'm gay."

Glistening tears trickled down Elly's cheeks. "I knew that's what you were going to say," she said.

"You have to believe me, I'm not telling you this because I want to go out and have affairs with men or anything. But I've been keeping this to myself since I was little. I love *you*. I thought that by now, at this stage in our lives, in our marriage, I could trust you to understand. That you would know my love for you is true and that this doesn't change who I am. I'm the same person you've always known. You just didn't know *this*. I want you to know every last part of me, of who I am."

(Even as I write these words, I see now how foolish my thinking was. You can't tell your wife you're gay and expect her to be perfectly fine with it. Who the hell was I_trying to bullshit? Of course I wanted affairs with other men—I'd already been testing the waters. Sex between myself and Elly had never satisfied me. Fuck, we hadn't had sex in months! I was lucky to get lucky on New Years Eve—once a year! Was it all because of me? No. I tried. I honestly tried.)

Elly had not been responding to my advances for months, not because of me, but because she had someone else in her life already. I know that now, but I was like a buffoon cartoon character then, you know the one, '*Dah. Which way did he go*?' I was dumb like that. I was easily fooled. I was self-absorbed, and that didn't help me see things for what they were with her, or what I was doing myself.

"Back in the '70s," I went on explaining, "I remember having a heavy crush on Robert F. Logan's character, Zechariah Coop, in *Across The Great Divide*. I couldn't have been more than 8-years-old," I told Elly. "I didn't know what those feelings were back then, but I know what they are now. But don't think even for a second that I don't love you. *I* chased *you*, remember? I didn't put all my effort into you for nothing. Do you understand?" I asked her.

She nodded, but as usual, as it had been with us right from the start, from those days of parking in her parents' cars, Elly didn't really reciprocate. I never knew how much of what I was saying she understood. I never knew how much she agreed with, or disagreed with. She never let me into that mind of hers. How in the world had we managed all those years together? I'd been doing all the sharing of mind, body, and spirit; and all I ever got back from Elly…was Elly.

I could see my one-way conversation was done. The air had cooled even more since we'd first arrived at the park. So why, as we headed back up to the car, did I think we were okay? I don't know. Hell, I'd dropped the bomb. This was the big one. There was no taking it back. I'd launched the first missile that day. Sometimes, even now, I wish I could return to the moment before I'd told Elly, and maybe not tell her. I know it wouldn't have changed what was inevitable, but at least she wouldn't have been able to use my own bomb against me. And that is just what she would do. In the most despicable fashion undreamt of by me—Undreamt.

Honky Dory

Timing: sometimes the timing of things in our lives is perfect. Sometimes, however, the timing is so wrong. Take, for instance, my timing in choosing to out myself to my wife. Can you say, Oooops! That word's going to be my next tattoo—across my fucking forehead.

Business went on as usual. I don't know if I was too preoccupied with myself to notice what was happening between Elly and me. That was the problem: there was no Elly and me. When she wasn't home working, she was gone to the Serpentarium with Hunter. It was ridiculous. But was it as ridiculous as me looking up Wesly's number in the phone book because I couldn't stop thinking about him? He was just as glad to hear from me as I was to have found him again. With that call, he'd given me an invite to come over one night and watch a movie, or something. I was sure to take him up on it.

In the weeks that followed, I found myself at Wesly's every third weekend or so. We thoroughly enjoyed one another's company. He was being cautious with me since I was a married man and all. He gave me the opportunity to spill my guts, and in doing so, finding out that he'd shared many of my experiences growing up. He was living in his own house: a small but tastefully decorated place for him and his adopted son. Usually by the time I arrived at night, his six-year-old was fast asleep. I didn't really get to know his son. And when it came time for intimacy, I was quite receptive to Wesly.

I had long needed to be comforted by someone in my life; Elly had never taken on that role. She was not the type to cuddle, kiss, or hold hands. The only time I'd ever heard her tell me she loved me was when I'd said it first. We hardly ever argued in all our years together, and when we did Elly liked to scream and walk away. Sex with Elly never happened without a week of hinting beforehand. If I didn't initiate it, we would have never had it. She just didn't seem interested in sex, whereas I was ready 24-7.

My family was under the impression that ours was the most successful union out of all of them. Little did they know how robbed of love and affection I felt. I remember the one and only time Elly and I held hands while out shopping. It was at a mall in St.Catharines. I reached to hold her hand as many of the couples passing us by were. And for the five minutes that we did hold hands, it felt unnatural (to both of us). The first excuse to let go, we did, and didn't attempt to try it again. *That* was our marriage.

Even though I loved her ever so deeply, even though she'd become my wife, I always suspected that Elly never quite got past our years as friends. Perhaps if we'd married as lovers instead of best friends, our roles as husband and wife would have been easier to play. And now she was searching for affection in the arms of another man—and so was I.

One night at Wesly's, he and I were sitting side by side on his sofa, watching television—but not really. He turned to me and said, "Well, if you're not gonna make the first move, I will."

And in taking my right hand into his, I could have wept. He fondled my palm with his fingers, so gently, so erotically. I felt weakened by the comfort of him. That was our only contact that night, holding hands. Whenever I got home from his place, my family would be asleep. I'd enter into the darkness of our bedroom, slip into bed, and wonder about everything.

I think my nights at Wesly's were usually Wednesdays, since Elly was gone every weekend. Probably three weeks past until my next visit to his house. I brought one of my photo albums along to show him what my children looked like. He held my hand again, but this time, I'd asked him to kiss me. His kiss lasted about half an hour. With our tongues dancing together, he showed me that there were ways to be kissed I'd never known. At one point, a shiver ran up and down my spine—shiver isn't the right word for what I felt—Zing! I thought about that kiss all the way back to

Welland, as I drove home aching hard.

In the daylight, more lies. I reassured Elly that Wesly was just a friend and that we were just watching movies together, and she reassured me that the weekends at the Serpentarium was just something to do. We were comfortable in our bullshit, pulling away from one another as though we couldn't help it. And maybe we couldn't. While she continued to spend all her weekends with her 'friends,' I continued to explore life with my 'friends.'

One night, by some odd coincidence, Elly and I were both home. I was lying in bed with the TV on and a psychology book on my lap. Elly entered the room with a towel wrapped around her, tucked under her arms. Standing on her side of the bed, she actually spoke to me.

"I think I might have to get this checked out," she said. I looked up to see her showing me the chestnut-sized lump above her left breast.

"Oh shit. What the hell is that?" I said.

"Feel it," she said, "it's really hard. It's not like those little duct things I get."

She was right. The lump was something else this time.

"You'd better show it to Liam right away," I said. "Don't freaking wait."

"I'm calling tomorrow," said Elly, slipping into bed next to me.

Happy Fucking New Year!

Another year's end was approaching. It was a lifeless year for me. I had dreamt my way through its' days and nights, pondering what kind of future was in store. Careless in my choices and oblivious to Elly's choices. Wesly had purchased tickets for he and I to attend his employer's Christmas Gala. I'd said yes, before I knew that Mona had also asked Elly to attend the same gala with her. She, Wesly, Brian, Bi, my cousin Michelle, and many of my clients were all employees of this major company. I lost my nerve and phoned Wesly to back out.

I explained my excuse in this way: "Many of my clients will be there. My cousin. My sister and her husband. Elly and her sister Mona… I just don't know where or how I would fit into the mix. What role am I supposed to play? Husband? Your Boyfriend? I can't do it. I'm not prepared for that situation. I wouldn't know who I was," I told him.

Wesly seemed to understand, or perhaps he didn't feel like dealing with my bullshit. Whatever the case, he said he'd have no problem finding someone else to use the ticket. I went with Elly to pick the black dress she would wear. I chose the glittery purse, too, which she chose later not to use (probably because I'd chosen it). Over the years, I'd purchased a lot of Elly's clothes, purses and shoes. Suddenly, my taste wasn't good enough for her.

She and Mona spent the night in the Niagara Falls hotel, where the gala was held. Bi and Steve saw them at one point, and the funny thing is, Steve thought Elly was having an affair since I wasn't there. His misunderstanding of that night was not as far-fetched as it seemed. I was glad once the dance was history. It just felt wrong to me. Elly and I should have been there together, or not at all.

Meanwhile, Lee had finally moved on after a seven month stint with us. He'd found a nice apartment on Lincoln Street. We didn't see him for Christmas. My family was undecided in whose house we were going to have our yearly get-together. No one was volunteering so I stepped up. Like Richard, I loved having the family at my house. I remember borrowing extra tables and chairs, which we really didn't use on the night of. Everyone seemed to be enjoying themselves, everyone except Elly. I barely saw her while our company was over. At one point, she was sitting in the wreck room with the little kids, instead of with the rest of the adults. I called for her to come and join us, but she mumbled something and didn't budge. When Debbie wanted to take photos of each couple that night, Elly just stood next to me, as if we'd forced her to pose. I saw the picture later, and you could tell she was disgusted to be next to me. Her arms were at her sides, her body leaning away from mine.

Unfortunately, that was not the only photograph of us together like that. There are many in our collection. My arms are around my wife's shoulders; my wife's arms are at her sides. It would seem I was blind to what even photographs were telling me loud and clear. She may have been the love of my life, but I was not hers. I never fully realized just how far from happiness we were.

Although Elly's smile didn't make an appearance at our Christmas party, I was sure to see it before she left for the Serpentarium with Hunter on New Years Eve. Taylor, Randee, Chanel, and I would spend that night just the four of us…again. We watched movies, ate junk food, drank soda, and were asleep before midnight. I had never spent New Years without Elly. She didn't think twice about not spending it with me. I was already nonexistent to her.

Within the first two weeks of January 2007, having grappled with the decision of whether or not I should come out to my family, I made a choice. It seemed to me now, that in sharing my secret with Elly, I hadn't done her any favor. I felt as though my initial idea of passing on the secret of my soul to her, as an act of greatest love, had proved to be nothing more than the handing over of my bag of bricks for her to bear. So, on our way to St. Catharines, our favorite shopping grounds for second-hand stores, I tried to remove a brick from Elly's bag by coming out to Beverly.

"Elly's the only one that knows this," I started to tell her. "I guess I've always known, but I never told anyone. I couldn't."

"Told what, Mike? I don't know what you're talking about?" said Bev.

"I know. Give me a second. This isn't easy to say. I guess I've..." I sighed.

"It's me—Bev. You know you can always tell me anything."

"I think I'm a little bit..."

Seeing that I just couldn't bring myself to say the word, Beverly finished for me.

"Gay?" she asked. "So, I don't care about that. You're my brother, Mike. I'll always love you no matter what. You're my best friend. You're the only man in my life that I love with all my heart. So what if you're gay. I have lots of gay friends."

I was trembling. I didn't know why I was so afraid to tell her. I loved her too. I knew she wouldn't let me down. I knew she wouldn't hate me. I knew I could count on Beverly to be Beverly.

About four days later, while driving with Bi in her truck, I knew it was time to share with her as well. I thought that with each person I told it would get easier, but it didn't. Instead, I choked up even more, always waiting for the negative response I'd been expecting my entire life. That didn't happen with Bi. Bi was soft in her reaction to my words. Like Beverly, she reminded me that we were brother and sister, and that nothing about me could change that fact. Nothing could take an ounce of love away from our relationship.

I'd gone from my oldest sister to my youngest sister, and their reactions were the same: they loved me. However, both sisters gave me the same advice in saying: don't tell anyone else, especially Mom—it would kill her. The one person whose reaction I could not get was Richard's. (*Even on this very day in May 2008, I wept in wondering if he would have stopped loving me for my gayness.*) Against the advice of my two sisters, I would soon steal more bricks from Elly's bag.

Brace Yourselves

On Friday, January 12, 2007, Elly had her breast lump removed, which by now had rapidly grown to the size of a golf ball. I was feeling overwhelmed with sadness for us. Our bills were strangling us. My coming out had flogged us. I'd fooled myself into believing I would be clear on who I was, but I was more confused than ever.

Brian called me during the first week of February. Said he was taking Wesly to see a comedy act at the casino and asked me to come along. Little did I know, there would be a fourth passenger with us. Wesly informed me that he was not too keen on this fourth person. He didn't seem like he was interested in Brian's belated birthday gift, either. I was riding shotgun in Brian's car that night. We picked up Brian's surprise addition first, pulling into the parking lot of an apartment building. Jacob, or Jay, climbed into the back seat. The first thing I noticed about him was that just like Brian, Wesly, and myself, Jay was soft-spoken.

I turned in my seat to shake his hand and introduce myself. Jay wasn't a good-looking man. He was the tallest of us, with dark hair parted to one side. I found his voice a bit annoying. His tones were all over the place, rising and falling like he was unsure whether he wanted to be masculine or feminine. Deep lows that almost sounded angry, then whispered highs that drifted off. Or perhaps my judgment of him was being unfairly manipulated by Wesly's warnings.

As we drove next to pick up Wesly, Jay seemed nice enough. He was employed as a nurse and lived on his own. Only a few years older than I, he seemed much older at first. I laughed to myself in knowing how Wesly felt about Jay, and him having to sit in the back seat next to him. Once we arrived at the casino, Brian broke the news to us: our tickets were for seats that weren't together. He and Wesly would be in the lower seats together, while Jay and I would have to sit in the balcony seats, in separate rows.

I was in a sillier-than-usual mood that night, trying to forget my worries. My over-the-top humor never fails to attract the wrong type of people. Jay, whom I was not purposely attempting to attract, flipped the tab for our first and only drinks. His gazing eyes made me uncomfortable, and I was glad to be sitting a few rows higher than he was. A young couple was sitting next to me. I was embarrassed, thinking to myself that they might believe I was Jay's partner. The show ran for about two hours. Then we met up and watched Brian play a few slot machines. Jay ran into one of his nieces, who'd been a one-time client of mine. I knew I'd never see her again after that night, and I was right. Jay told me how she'd asked him what I—a married man with children—was doing with three queers. *Wasn't it obvious*? I thought. *Gambling*!

After that night, Brian confided in me that he'd been rather disappointed with Wesly. "He didn't seem to appreciate the show," he said.

There were other matters causing friction between them, dividing their friendship. I didn't tell Brian that I'd been seeing Wesly. Nothing much was going on between us anyway. The same woman who was leaving his house in the van on the night we met was quickly becoming a giant wedge between us. I would drive all the way to Wesly's, only to find myself keeping company with *myself*. Wesly would be on the phone for most of my visit, talking with his lesbian *fag-hag*. I didn't learn that term until we went clubbing over the border.

His conversations with her made me angry. I could only visit with him once every couple of weeks, and there he was, gabbing on the phone with her the entire time. I became outright rude toward her near the end, and they thought I was being humorous. He'd already told me that his last partner left him on account of her (guess he didn't get the hint). Now she was pushing the idea of her and her two boys moving in with Wesly! She wasn't getting along with her lesbian girlfriend and was looking for an easy out. Wesly would have been insane to let her move into his tiny house with him and his son. I wasn't too concerned, however; whatever interest I'd first held for Wesly, she was helping diminish.

Back home, tension between Elly and I was gelling. As I readied myself to go out one day, Elly was in the front porch sorting out coats. I went in to take my coat off its hook and put it on. When Elly turned to leave the porch room, I blocked her exit, smiling, and reaching to hug her. She kept dodging side to side, trying to avoid me. I giggled and said, "What are you doing? Stop acting like you hate me."

Elly's eyes narrowed, her brow furrowed, and her lips pursed. "I—DO—HATE—YOU," she said, teeth grinding.

The words sounded so absurd to me, I just chuckled for a second. Then I realized she was completely sincere with her intent to get me the fuck away from her.

"You hate me?" I echoed, stepping aside to let her pass.

"That's right. I *hate* you. You're an asshole."

I zipped my coat up, smiling no more, and as I headed for the door, said, "Thanks a lot. Real nice."

After that day her silence began. This type of behavior was far from new to me, since Mr. East had perfected the art of Silent-Treatment. That man could go years without speaking a single word to those who were supposed to be his loved ones. I'd always considered such treatment to be cruel and heartless—wicked. Elly, it seemed, had purchased a membership to the S.T. Club, and was performing like a pro.

She could pass me by twenty times in the day, and not a sound came from her. I was invisible. It hurt like hell and made me depressed, but she carried it on for so long, I eventually got used to it—not really. She was spending more and more of her nights at the Serpentarium, and as little time as possible with the kids and me. I was amazed on the night she finally spoke to me again, only to tell me we had to drive to St. Catharines the next day to hear the results of the tests performed on her tumor. It wasn't exactly a date to go for ice-cream.

On our way to meet with the cancer specialist, I asked Elly if there was something I should know about her and the snake guy. She said no, but by the way she shrugged her left shoulder, half smirked, shifted in her seat uncomfortably, and hard-pressed herself against the door, I knew the true answer was yes. Hell, if not for the door, Elly would have slid right out of the car. We drove the rest of the way in silence.

When we arrived in the parking lot of the specialist's office, I waited in the car, while Elly went inside on her own. Moments later, she knocked at the passenger window and yelled, "She wants you to come in for a minute."

"Why?" I yelled.

"Because it's not good news."

I remember swallowing hard as if I had a mouthful of peanut butter. I followed Elly into the tiny office, where other patients were sitting by the door, staring up at us like we'd entered the chamber of doom. We walked straight into the doctor's office, where she closed the door behind us. She was a pretty woman. I think I shook her hand. Elly and I sat in chairs facing the doctor's desk. I don't know how many words she spoke before the big 'C' word rang in my ears. After that, I fell out of reality as she continued to describe the types of treatments she planned to give Elly.

Certain bits of her talking would scream into my mind, like when she told us that Elly's cancer was a rare, fast traveling type, which she'd only dealt with about four times previously. Elly even asked her how well those patients had fared. Her response: only one had survived. She told Elly she hoped to give her as many years to live as possible. However, the cancer had already made its way into the lymph nodes under Elly's left arm. Elly would have to have a mastectomy.

The doctor left us alone for a few minutes to digest the news together, but we weren't together. I hid my face in my hands and wept, and Elly, she pat my shoulder the instant the doctor re-entered the room. I felt like shit. It was Elly's moment to be consoled, but I wasn't the one she wanted to be comforted by. She barely knew how to give comfort to me.

I couldn't stop the tears as I drove us back to Welland. I don't remember seeing Elly cry. She was probably in shock. I dropped her off and headed right to Brian's house. We were sitting about two feet from one another as I told him what had happened. "She hates me," I said, collapsing into sobs.

Brian placed his right hand on my left shoulder and squeezed. "It's okay, Mike," he soothed.

I only stayed long enough to stop crying. I thanked him for listening to me whine again, and headed over to see Mom. We hugged, Mom and I, and cried, and then I returned home. I just wanted to hold Elly, tell her I loved her, lend what little strength I had left to her, but that wouldn't happen. I don't even recall where she was when I got home. I think she went out the side door as I entered the back door. I'm sure someone comforted her that night, but it wasn't me.

On February 21, Elly went in for the mastectomy. Mr. East brought her because my wife was having nothing to do with me. This was the beginning of her shutting me out of everything to do with her and her treatments. She stayed in the hospital overnight but was home the next day. I was under the impression that she was in for a hell of a recovery period. But the very next night, Elly went to see her snake man. I couldn't believe it. Everyone was so worried about her, and there she was already on the go—the next fucking night!

As for me, I went to see Lee at his new apartment. I wanted so much to tell him my secret, but I couldn't bring myself to do it. I was terrified of losing a friend. I started to tell him, but then changed my mind, leaving him wondering. A few days later, when we were speaking on the phone, I tried to brave it again, and again I was stalling. Lee figured it out on his own.

"You like cats and dogs," he said, joking.

That was it. He didn't spit names at me or hang up. He accepted it and we went on with our friendship like nothing had changed. He has no idea how grateful I was to him for that moment of normalcy.

About a week later, I found myself sitting in Liam's office, a pack of shot nerves. I had something to tell him, and it wasn't what he already knew pertaining to Elly's situation. I apologized and apologized to him. I'm not sure for what—keeping my secret, perhaps. I'm certain Liam had already clued into my secret, after all, he had given me a physical, and I had no control over how I'd reacted to being exposed. Like I said, I'm positive Liam had some sort of idea about me.

"I'm sorry I never told you. Elly knows now. I told her back in October. I thought we were okay, but we're finished. She... hates my guts. I haven't even told my mother yet," I explained, without saying anything.

Liam's eyes always seemed to stare right into me like he knew what I was thinking. I felt compelled to tell him.

"I'm...I'm..." I stuttered like I was that kindergarten kid again, lying to Mom about my wet pants.

"What?" Liam said. "What is it? I'm here for you. No matter how bad you think it is, I'm here for you. You know that. You don't have to be afraid to tell me anything."

I started again, tears welling in my eyes. "I'm..."

"You're what? Having an affair?" he tried to guess.

"No. It's not that. You know already. I know you do. I'm... I'm..."

"Gay," Liam finished.

Tears began to rush forth as if a fire hose had been shoved up my ass. I nodded as Liam came around his desk to sit next to me. He put his hand on my back. "I'm proud of you. That took a lot of guts to tell me. I'm glad you did. It's okay, Mike. You haven't done anything wrong. I understand how you feel," he said.

When I left Liam's office that day, I didn't feel any better than I had when I'd gone in. Not because of anything Liam did or didn't do; he was a good doctor, a good counselor, and a good friend. But because I still carried the pain of everything that was now my life. (Yeah, some life.)

Don't Mind Me, You Keep Partying

Then came my big night out in March. Wesly had convinced Brian to take us to Buffalo, where, as I'd been told, all the gay clubs were. I told Elly where we were going, I just didn't tell her *where* we were going. Brian picked me up and brought me back to his house, where we waited for Wesly to meet us. When Wesly came down into the basement, I remember looking at him and thinking, *what do I see in him?* He wasn't very attractive.

He and I certainly did not act as though we'd been hanging out together. Brian handed him a beer, which he guzzled down before I was finished mine. The three of us grabbed our coats and left for Buffalo in Brian's car. I gave him gas money but Wesly never chipped in, which was something I thought he should have done, since the trip was **his** idea.

We stopped at the Duty Free shop and changed our Canadian money into American. At the border, Brian handed me his ID to hold for him, as did Wesly. I laughed at their photos, but especially at Wesly's. Brian looked good in his photo, but Wesly's was terrible. Again, I found myself wondering what it was that had attracted me to him.

From the border, we drove about ten minutes before we reached our first destination: a small bar that served 'the best cocktails around.' I felt so awkward in that place. I looked around at the other people, but no one stuck out of the crowd. They were just other people like us (queers out for a social drink). I was there. I was one of them. Yeah. I was one of them. We took our jackets off and hung them on hooks behind us. I made the mistake of being the only one dressed like a queer. I'd put on this shiny black silk top I had. I liked the way the material felt on my skin, and thought it would be a cool top to wear for dancing. My jacket was a leather rip-off but everyone liked it.

Wesly paid for our first round of cocktails. He'd been correct in describing the drinks as the best anywhere. From large glasses, we sipped them rather quickly and went on to seconds. That was about the time when two faces, familiar to Wesly and Brian, walked in. One was a short young Italian, wearing a coat similar to my own. His friend was a much older man, with his most striking feature being that of his white Einstein hairdo. Neither fellow was particularly attractive. Brian introduced me to the pair, since Wesly was behaving too excitedly to bother.

Two more queers entered the bar, followed by their hefty lesbian friend. The young Italian stared at them with discontent. He turned to us and said, "Fucking queers. Why don't they leave their fag-hags at home. I hate that. I can't stand having women in the bars I go to. It's supposed to be men only. Fuck."

Brian casually turned to face me, his right eye cocked. He later warned me to ignore Mack's comments, saying, "Mack's a women hater. He says shit like that all the time. Guy's got issues."

We stayed for a third cocktail, and then Wesly insisted we move on to the next bar on such-and-such a street. In the car, Wesly was high on the night. He rambled on about how many people he knew in Buffalo, and how many knew him. He was having his own private reunion with the gay community. Once we parked, it was revealed to me just how many gay bars were lined up in a row on this particular street. You could literally step out one door and into the neighboring one. My annoyance with Wesly was just about to heighten.

We entered our second bar with our two new additions following. For the first few minutes things were all right. I was getting to know the two new guys, while Brian smiled a lot, and Wesly made it known to us how many guys he was finding attractive in the bar. The younger guy, Mack, was showing an interest in me. He was surprised to learn that Wesly and I had been sort of seeing each other. I was insulted when Wesly described our relationship as an 'on again, off again' thing. *What was that supposed to mean*? I thought. As far as I was aware, we were always on. Guess he wanted us to be off that night.

Once Wesly walked away, Mack had to move in close to me to yell above the music, "What do you see in *him*?" he asked.

"Not much!" I yelled back. "Every time I'm at his place, he's on the phone the whole night with this fat lesbian friend of his. I swear they might as well be a couple themselves."

"He ignores you for *Her*?!" Mack shouted. "What an asshole. Fuck him. You're too good for him anyway. Don't you think he's too good for Wes?" he questioned his Einstein friend.

Einstein nodded and said, "Oh yeah. You're really good-looking. Don't waste your time on someone like Wes." That's when Einstein noticed the tribal tattoo around my collar bone. "Is that real?" he asked me.

"Yeah," I said, opening my shirt wider to reveal more of the design.

Mack stepped right in, gently running his fingers down the tattoo, saying, "Did that hurt?"

"Only on the collar bones," I said.

Spotting Brian at the bar, I leaned in to tell Mack I'd been harboring a small crush on Brian. This raised his brows again. However, I also told him that Brian wasn't interested in me. That he'd spoken of some nameless other in Toronto, who he'd met on line. Mack shook his head.

"That's bullshit! He has no one. And you're way better looking than his last boyfriend—oh fuck yeah. Way better looking!" he said as he turned to watch a couple of queers walk in with their hefty lady friends. "Fuck I hate that. Fucking fag-hags."

But Mack wasn't the only one trying to get closer to me that night. His friend, whose name I never did catch, was also moving into my comfort zone. The way his gentle eyes looked right through me, I felt I could trust this man. I soon learned that I wasn't the only one present who had children. He'd also been married, had kids, and was divorced. I knew he was also attracted to me, but he wasn't pushy like Mack, and before the night was over, Mack would push too far.

While in that bar, I couldn't finish my drink, nor did I order one in the next. As I was standing against the wall with Einstein, a heat-wave rushed from my toes, up to the top of my head. I felt like I'd been zapped by electricity. "Woe. Something weird just happened to me," I told him. "Tell Brian and Wesly I had to step out for some air."

I left the bar and hustled across the street to where we'd parked the car. Brian's doors were locked. I looked back at the bar but did not see my friends coming out, so I began to slowly walk up and down the ice-covered sidewalk. It was freezing in Buffalo, and I was hating my choice in dress. A Negro girl, who was cutting across the street toward me, observed, "You look lost."

I smiled and assured her that I wasn't.

By the time Brian and Wesly did find me, I was hoping they'd know enough to cut the evening short and take me home. No such luck. Wesly was very adamant about which bars to hit next. We pulled into our next stop, which was a flashy bar with neon lights around the entrance. I told them to go on in without me. I needed time to get a hold of myself. Wesly practically ran from the car. Brian kept asking me if I was okay. They blamed my queasiness on the alcohol, but I insisted that it wasn't. They were under the impression that I'd had five drinks, as they had. But I'd only had three drinks, and what I was feeling did not seem alcohol related to me.

Brian had no sooner left me alone, when I had to open the door and vomit. In my effort to keep his car clean, I'd splashed puke on my sleeve. There was a brief moment of relief afterward, but it only lasted a few minutes. I went inside the bar to find a washroom to clean my jacket and find my friends. A bouncer stopped me and informed me that there was a cover charge; I had to pay to rinse my fucking sleeve. Once I came out of the washroom, I found Brian standing behind Wesly. They were watching amateurs dance on a stage.

Wesly was dancing by himself, dancing and clapping, happy in his own little world. Brian smiled at me and again asked if I was okay. That's when a midget, dressed in a black leather bondage outfit, came out onto the stage to shake her thang to Christina

Aguilara's "Dirty!" I couldn't believe what I was seeing. When her act was done, Brian had to grab Wesly by the arm and drag him out. But that wasn't the end of it. We got in the car and drove to the *next* bar. I'd have to say that out of the string of dumps we'd been in, this next one was the worst.

Brian handed me a bottle of water he'd bought for me. I was grateful. Our old friends, Mack and Einstein, were already at this bar. I joined them all on the tiny dance-floor, where Wesly immediately began to shadow-dance behind another guy. I think I managed to squeeze in two songs, then I was done. I had no energy left to carry on pretending that I felt fine. In fact, my body was telling me to find the washroom…and fast!

I looked around but I didn't see any washroom signs. Between the fat woman who was standing right at the edge of the dance-floor, watching the gay guys, and the tall blond creepy guy who wouldn't stop staring at me, I needed to get out of there. I asked Brian where the washroom was, but Mack interrupted his response. "I'll take you," he volunteered.

He led me around the bar counter, past a couple groups of people huddled together, to the back hallway. I wasn't comfortable with this already, being out of sight from my friends, well, so-called friends. The washroom's roughly plastered walls were painted whorehouse red. I headed into the farthest stall, but froze when I saw the pile of human shit on the floor in front of the toilet. Before I could exit that stall, Mack pushed himself inside with me. I looked down to make sure I wasn't about to decorate my shoes with feces. Mack and I were face to face, barely a foot apart.

"What are you doing?" I asked him.

"I'm coming in with you," he answered.

"While I take a shit?"

Without another word, Mack's face disappeared behind his wide-open mouth that was about to consume me. Being an amateur at handling public washroom violations, I allowed my closed lips, my nose, and half my face to dip into the darkness of his trap. Then I calmly pushed him back, squeezing my way past him and out of the 'shitty' stall. I sat on the filthy counter as he apologized, but I wasn't really listening to the idiot. Brian suddenly appeared around the corner, staring at me from the hallway. I gave him a look with rolling eyes that said, *Don't you dare leave me alone with this freak.* Brian must have understood because he remained with me until Mack left us.

"Did he try something?" Brian whispered.

"Someone should have warned him that I'd just puked before he tried to suck my whole fucking head inside his mouth," I said.

Brian chuckled and said, "He tried to kiss you?"

If not for feeling so sick, I might have been able to see the humor of it all. Instead, my anger toward Wesly was gaining ground. After all, none of this would have happened if we'd left earlier. Brian and I left the washroom to return to the others. I saw an old sofa facing the front door, which was ajar. So I flopped down on it, letting the cold air cover me like a blanket. Face-sucker-Mack came and sat next to me for a moment to make a more sincere apology. Without ever looking at him, I told him it was okay. *Moron*, I thought.

Early morning had sneaked up on us. I couldn't tell what time it was because the bars never closed. Brian yanked me up off of the sofa saying, "Come on, Mike, we're going."

I thought he meant we were going home. Had he finished his sentence, it would have ended with, *we're going for breakfast and you'll just have to suffer for another hour or so.*

We entered a brightly lit, open-all-night restaurant. Seems no one in Buffalo knows when to get their asses to bed. Nor did a group of four Canadian queers, myself not included, of course. Brian, Wesly, Mack, and Einstein ordered huge plates of eggs, bacon, toast, and coffee. When I saw those forks digging into those eggs... I vanished once more, hiding away in the washroom—the first and only clean washroom of the night. While I was sitting with my ass on the toilet, I watched through the crack of the stall door as a sharply dressed Negro took a few snorts of his powder. Our eyes met for an instant, but he didn't seem bothered by me in the least. He checked his jacket in the mirror and left.

I returned to our table but didn't mention what I'd seen. My

Canadian buddies were too busy shoveling down their meals and poking fun about Einstein's apparent nine inches. Mack made a joke at my expense; I think he was feeling bitter, don't you? When Brian purposely mentioned how I'd barfed at the bar just previous to the last one, you should have seen Mack's face.

"You puked?" he said.

I nodded. *Sometimes it just doesn't pay to be a prick*, I thought.

"You must really be sick," Wesly added, "or you'd have all kinds of comebacks."

I couldn't believe my ears. It had taken an entire night for Wesly to realize I was sick?! That did it for me. Having heard enough of their juvenile table-talk, I excused myself and left the building. I was probably outside for twenty minutes, before Brian finally came out to unlock his car doors for me. He turned the heat on and covered me with his jacket.

"Wesly's almost done. I'm really sorry it's taking so long, Mike," he said.

Brian's apology sounded nice, but I couldn't help feeling just as angry toward him as I did toward Wesly for my undeserved suffering. I would have never put one of them through a night like I'd had. They'd been selfish. He'd been correct in telling me Wesly was nearly finished because they came out moments later. Wesly was as hyper at the end of the night as he'd been at its start. I closed my eyes and listened to the two of them talk all the way back to Welland, and home. I don't know what any of them thought about me that night, or spoke behind my back, but I would never go out with them again.

Turned out I'd been correct in my self-diagnosis, too. Alcohol was not at the core of my illness; I had caught a Flu bug. Tammy and her son, Timmer, had also spent the same weekend with all the same symptoms as I had. I laid in bed for three days. I should have told Brian how pissed at him I was, but I couldn't bring myself to do it, for fear I'd scare him off. On the other hand, that's exactly what I did with Wesly. Brian had phoned me that Saturday to see how I was feeling. Even Mack had phoned me, trying to hook up. I pretended to take his number down during our conversation, but

I had no intention to meet up with him again.

Now Wesly, having been closest to me, should have been the first to check on me; however, he waited until Monday night to call.

"You sound angry," he'd said to me.

"I am! You treated me like shit. Not once did you bother to ask if I was okay. All you were worried about was which bar we were going to hop to next. It was all about you that night," I told him.

"I was just trying to show you what the 'gay' life was like," he said in his defense.

"Well, that's not *my* 'gay' life," I replied.

Our conversation ended somewhere along those lines. The bastard didn't apologize, either. When next I tried to phone him, he wouldn't answer my calls. Man, was I fuming. This was not the person I thought I was getting to know. The next time I saw Wesly, I'd stopped in while I was in St. Catharines with Tammy. I'd lent him a copy of my poetry book to read, so I had no choice but to go back for it. He smiled at me when he opened the door.

"What are you doing here?" he asked. Not in a miserable tone, but as a regular question.

"I just came for my book," I said.

As I stood there, Wesly went into the living room to scold his son about how rough he was playing with his toys. I stared at him, wondering why I'd never noticed the size of his belly before now. He was a short guy, and that belly was looking about nine months pregnant! I guess maybe it is true what people say: that most times we see beyond a person's appearance when we're attracted to their personalities. The opposite can be said about relationships once the inner attraction subsides: that's when we start to judge a person's physical attributes. I guess it makes it easier for us to break up.

He returned to the kitchen, where I was still waiting. I noticed his eyes avoiding mine.

"You're not still mad at me are you?" I asked him.

"Na. I'm over it," he said.

"See you later," I said, and closed the door.

As I walked down his driveway toward Tammy's car, I thought, *He's Over It*?! *Acts like he's the one who'd been treated like shit. Never see* ***him*** *again.* And I never have.
Brian and I had taken in another movie, but I was feeling so bitter, when I opened my mouth, nothing impressive came out. I called him the next night to apologize, saying, "I'm drunk with depression and don't quite know what I'm saying anymore."

I really must have left a bad impression because I'd recently expressed my interest in accompanying him on a trip to New York; however, after the movie night, he told me he now had someone else in mind to go with. I couldn't blame him. I was a mess. There were much worse things happening than Brian's rejection. I'd had another 'boohoo' session with Liam. He always seemed to understand me. He knew I was feeling lonely and confused about who I was. My sadness was devastating.

Elly was expected to begin her chemo treatments, but after discovering that her white blood-cell count was too low, they delayed treatment for at least two weeks. It wasn't good. By the end of March, Elly had finally started treatment. They were administering a medication to keep her blood-cell count up between each chemo treatment. She was well enough. If ever she felt sick, I didn't see it. I must have been so detestable to her during those days, she couldn't bear to be home. One day I told her I missed her; she said nothing in response. I was learning to live differently—lonely. Her silence was **my** cancer.

Forty-Five Dollars!

APRIL: I don't know when the phone calls started, but Brian had tossed my number into Jay's hands. Yes, Jay (the casino dude). He'd begun to call almost every day and night, asking me if I wanted to go out for wings and suck—Oops!—I mean, such. I kept making up excuses why I couldn't. Most of the time, Elly was at the Serpentarium and I was home with the girls. I wasn't about to leave them alone like their mother had no problem doing. But wouldn't you know it, I began to run into him all over the city. In the parking lot of a convenient store, in the mall, and then while I was out walking alone down Merritt Island.

There was no avoiding him on that walk, but as he allowed me to shed a few tears and whine about the avalanche state of my marriage, I'd found a good listener. He tried to comfort me with positive coaching and reassurance. I was hurting, and I was unable to conceal the pain any longer. Jay could see that. At one point during our stroll, when no one was around, he pulled me off the main path and gave me a gentle hug, saying, "You need a hug. I can tell. You'll be okay. Things will work out."

He squeezed my shoulders. "My God. You're all tensed up. I'm good at giving back rubs, you know. You'll have to try me some time."

At the end of the trail, we went our separate ways. The new sandals I'd just purchased had blistered my ankles and tore the skin off my heels. I had to walk home barefoot, carrying my lousy forty-five dollar sandals in my hand. But then it was I who could not stop thinking about Jay all the way home, and for the days to follow. He didn't phone me after that, not as I'd expected he might.

A few weeks later, I dug his number out and made the call to him. I left him a message on his answering-machine, and the following day, Jay returned my call. We agreed to meet for coffee that afternoon. Elly was home for once, so I was able to leave without worrying about the kids. I told her I was going for coffee.

Jay picked me up and drove us back to his apartment building on the north side of town. His apartment was tidy. As he stood in the kitchen, stirring our coffees, I noticed that there weren't any photographs of family, or anyone. We sat down on his sofa, where he mentioned his up-and-coming birthday. I think he was going to be 42-years-old. I didn't care about the small talk. I didn't care that the coffee tasted like muddy water. I'd agreed to meet him because I was desperate; desperate for affection, for the touch of another, for intimacy, for the back rub he'd offered, and was hoping for more.

I put my steaming cup down and said, "So, you owe me a back rub."

Jay looked surprised. He sipped his coffee, put it down, and then said, "You're serious?"

"Hey, you're the one that was bragging."

"How's the coffee?" he asked me.

"It's good," I lied, removing my T-shirt.

"Oh, you want me to do it now," said Jay.

(CENCORED!)

Needless to say, I was soon dropped off back at my house, and although the experience wasn't all bad, well, let me just say that it wasn't very good, either. Jay turned out to be rather bizarre. Quite a bit larger in size and strength than I, he proved to be a little too desperate for my likings. I know, I know, I was supposed to be the desperate one. Had the two of us been rated for desperation on a scale from 1 to 10, I would have been a six or seven, while Jay would have been a twelve!

There were moments when all he did was stare into my eyes, behaving like some madman. He would move in close to kiss me, then pull back at the last second, as if we were playing some game only he was aware of. And the kisses themselves! Oh my god. I thought Mack's alien attack was gross. Jay's kisses gagged me. They weren't kisses; more like someone was ramming a wriggling eel into my mouth. (No wonder the guy's single.)

He'd given me one too many hugs, too, lifting me off my feet; I felt like I was a puppy in the death grip of an innocent child. My back actually hurt for a couple weeks after the fact. One moment he would be so gentle, and the next… One thing was clear to me: I didn't like the feeling of being the weaker of the two of us.

Jay, thinking things had gone super, kept calling me. I finally phoned him back and left the following message on his machine: "Hi, Jay, it's Mike. Listen, my life is too complicated right now. I need to get my head in order. There won't be any repeats of our last visit together. Okay. So…yeah, gimme a call sometime."

Jay was able to read between the lines, and he never phoned me again.

Now I'd done it. I'd kicked Wesly out of my life, Jay, Mack never got in, and only Brian was left. I was back to square one, as they say. My social life was right where it had begun—nowhere. I had no one to see during the weeks, and my weekends were spent with my twin girls and Chanel. The four of us would watch movies and eat junk food every Friday, Saturday, and Sunday night. I knew what was happening within our little family, but I was numb to everything.

April Fool

Everything that was going on with my life had taken its toll on my mother. She suffered a mild stroke. Mr. East, being the heartless prick that he is, dropped her off at the hospital, saying, "Call me when you're done."

For two days, I felt so dizzy I couldn't move my eyes. My blood-pressure reading was 177 over 103, which, apparently, is not good. When I told Elly about it, she simply replied, "Take an aspirin."

No wonder my head was spinning: Elly had finally admitted to her affair with the snake man. She no sooner confessed to me, when I learned from our children that she'd already been questioning them about who they wanted to live with! When the twins made it clear that they intended to stay with me, her anger toward them became evident. One afternoon, right in front of Lee and I, she screamed at Randee for spilling a drink in 'her' car, calling her a 'dumb bitch!' She then decided not to take any of the kids with her that day, stating, "Now you know why I don't want to take you guys with me, you're all assholes!"

Later, of course, she denied ever saying any of it. But that wouldn't be the last time she would cuss them out, or me. The night before my mother's birthday, April 24th, while soaking in the tub, I'd challenged God to rescue Elly from her dreaded disease, only to find myself being accused by her the next morning of trying to steal her clients. Once she had exhausted that topic, she switched to arguing about our lagging bills and lack of groceries. When I told her I was paying our bills and doing the best I could, she said, "You're best isn't good enough!"

We were self-employed hairstylists in a small community. Without her income, my income alone was not sufficient to keep things going. What I didn't know at the time was that Elly was already collecting a disability pension for her cancer. She must have been saving it for her big move because not a penny of it went into helping us out of our financial jam. I came to realize a lot about Elly in a short while, more than I ever knew in our lifetime together. We were in April, and I was her April fool.

Hunter was home sick the day we argued. He'd been upstairs, listening to everything. I felt so awful for him. I know what it's like to hear your parents argue. And that day, things reached a new level of intensity. From blaming me for the loss of her clients, which was no one's fault but her own, to accusing me of not working hard enough to pay the bills, Elly's anger was fully aimed in my direction. The instant I told her she'd been putting herself above her family, ignoring and mistreating her daughters, and flaunting her affair in front of her 11-year-old son, she started to fling dishes at me from the kitchen sink.

Four or five plates and bowls later, our entire dining room and salon floors were decorated with tiny pieces of shattered Correll (I thought Correll was supposed to be unbreakable). I'll never forget the hate within her eyes as she whipped those dishes. Then she made life worse for all of us by calling my step-father, Mr. East. She told him lies, which he in turn passed along to my mother and Bi. He told them that poor Elly had tried and tried to talk to me, but I would never listen, walking away from her. That I must have thrown something at her first to provoke her.

He had the nerve to think I would sit down with him, Mom, and Elly to discuss matters. In a million years I would never sit with him to discuss marital strife. This same man who'd recently called me a 'fucking faggot' to my nephew. And who, presently destroying his *third* marriage, thinks he can act as a counselor for mine. This man who tried to convince my mother and sister that Elly wasn't having an affair because…

"Kissing is not having an affair!"

I don't need to tell you how wrong that is. But it is clear why he goes through wives like families go through toilet-paper. Am I bitter? I'd tried and tried with Elly. I could finally accept the fact that this woman was not the woman I'd married. Not the person I'd fallen in love with in high school. Not the person I'd had four children with. Not my Elly. Nor, in all fairness to her, was I the man she'd married. I knew that. I understood what my coming out meant to her. The cancer followed. The boyfriend was there. Between myself and the disease, we gave her the perfect excuse to embrace this new Elly.

I understood the drama in her life, but only to a certain point. Then, I believe, the rest was her own folly. For her part, and worse than her absence, was Elly's treatment of the kids. She'd abandoned them. And every time she was leaving, Chanel would be left in tears, chasing Elly's speeding car up the road. She was crushing our seven-year-old's heart. Many of my clients could see what was going on. No one was blind to Elly's negligence. There were even days when Elly would be going somewhere with the three older kids, and still refuse to take Chanel along. Or she would phone the kids and tell them to sneak out and meet her at the store next to our house, without Chanel being aware. I didn't understand what reasoning could possibly be behind her cruelty. What was becoming of her, and why?

This woman whom I'd always admired for her strength and beauty was suddenly on a mission to destroy me. Her hatred toward me was growing ever more painful as each day opened my eyes to her deception and blatant disregard for the well-being of our children. Hunter and the twins confided in me one night, telling me Elly and her sister had told them I was gay. They had told my two 13-year-old daughters and my 12-year-old son that their father was gay.

"Does that mean when you told us we were gorgeous, you didn't mean it?" Taylor asked me. I felt so saddened by her confusion, and so *fucking* pissed off at Elly's stupidity. Now *she* was the April fool!

Part 3

Sickness In My Brain

The first weeks following Richard's death had been the lowest low in my life, until May of 2007. My days at their worst were my best. Mom had heard from Mr. East that Elly was trying to get Legal-Aid to rid herself of the garbage that was me. Bi had seen her in a store with her boyfriend; she pretended not to notice my sister. Bi told me all she could do was stand there and cry.

I'd been trying to hide my emotions from my family, but I was just so sad. At times, many times, I wished I didn't exist. I remember hoping that there wasn't an afterlife; one round of bullshit was enough. I even wished I was an alcoholic, so I could drown myself in my sorrows and disappear for a while. I no longer believed in hope or faith, but I believed in betrayal. I believed in the power of hate. I believed in what I could feel…like sadness. I believed I would remain alone forever, and that my hurt would never go away.

I hated Elly for killing a big part of me, for telling our kids that their dad was gay, for kissing another man in front of our son, and for turning our lives into trash without giving a fuck. I hated myself for everything else. I hated all the years I wasted believing in God, whispering prayers at night to no one. I hated myself for liking those who did not like me. I hated my mind, my body, and my spirit—if such a thing existed. I hated that my life had caused my family so much pain. I hated hate! I believed my life was shit!

I couldn't stop thinking about life, and how I didn't want anything to do with it. I thought about quitting every day. Suicide was all I could think about, as if it was a sickness in my brain. It was overwhelming me, all consuming, draining. There was no one I could tell this to without exposing my great weakness. I couldn't cry enough. I was faking wellness for my kids. Lee had moved back in with us, and even his presence made no difference. I was alone in my sadness. I was feeling more alone around others than I was on my own.

Elly had become a cruel joke on my life. The one day I finally heard her speaking with joy and excitement in her voice, she was cutting one of her new friend's hair, and talking about her boyfriend, while I was cutting hair not two feet from her. I wished I was nothing at that moment; nothing was better than being me, and alone.

Shifting The Weight

During May and June, I removed a couple more bricks from Elly's bag. I'd told Tammy my secret. We were driving in her car—yeah, I know, the car again, but cars are private. It wasn't any easier to tell her than it had been to tell Bev and Bi. Her son, Timmer, was riding in the seat behind me.

"Yes! It's about time!" he cheered. "Now I'm not the only one in the family."

Tammy shed a few tears and reached over to hug me, saying, "It's okay, Mike. It's all good, right."

Probably, my coming out meant more to those two than anyone else in the family. Timmer had taken years of pummeling from everyone for being gay, especially his own mother. And there I was the entire time, hiding. We all knew he was queer right from the start. That poor little boy, prancing around in his sister's dresses, so happy, so sweet, so punished for being what he was.

I'd always been a little envious of him. He grew up to be proud of himself, strong, with the attitude that if you didn't like him—fuck you! I wished I could be more like him. More…myself. Although my nephew is flamboyant and I am not, we are both gay. I love him so much. And I'm so proud of him. Not because he's gay, but because he's himself! And that day in Tammy's car, I understood what my being gay meant to him. We've been better friends ever since.

I hope you realize the importance of my including so much about Timmer here. I should have been his greatest support while he was growing up, but I wasn't. Instead, now, he is mine. I love and support you, Timmy West!

Mom was my next brick. The funny thing is, I really don't remember how she responded. I do know, however, that what I told her didn't quite set in the first time. She required additional, gentle convincing before she would accept what I was telling her. In the meantime, Lee had found a new girlfriend to hang with, and Elly came and went like our home was a variety store. When she was home, she wasn't home to me.

Her behavior with the kids became appalling. She argued with Chanel nearly every day about who she would have to live with. Chanel wanted to stay with me, but Elly kept telling her 'the judge was going to make her live with her.' There were times when I was working on a client, and Chanel would come to me in tears because Elly had yelled at her, arguing about who our daughter HAD to live with. It made me sick. I didn't understand it then, and I don't understand it now.

On several occasions, Elly came home late with the kids from her sister's house. Chanel would come straight to my room, where Lee and I were either asleep or watching TV (we were sharing the small wreck-room since Elly had taken over the main bedroom in the basement). The look on my baby girl's face broke my heart, when she described how Elly and Mona had sent the other kids out of the room to lecture her (Again) on what the Judge was going to make her do, reinforcing the idea that she wouldn't be allowed to live with her dad.

When Elly passed by the room, I called to her and asked, "What the heck are you trying to do to this kid?"

"What are YOU trying to do to her?!" she screamed. This was Elly as I'd never seen her before: completely convinced of her own hype. She went on about how I'd been 'brainwashing' our youngest child. No, I had no idea what the hell she was talking about, either. Seemed to me like what she and her sister were doing was an attempt to 'brainwash' Chanel. In any case, they'd only succeeded in strengthening Chanel's determination to stick with me.

On another occasion, Chanel was standing right beside us, when Elly shoved me and snapped a hand-towel in my face. The towel knocked something off a shelf and broke it. I made the decision to phone the police on her that day. She was becoming too comfortable attacking me physically, and the last thing I needed was to take on the role of abused husband in front of our children.

Chanel never forgot that incident. She brought it up to me a couple times afterward. Having called the police to our home invited Children's Aid—or FACS, as they are now called—to pay us a visit. At first I thought this woman from FACS was going to help us, but it quickly became clear whom she was willing to help. She sat with Lee, Elly, and myself at the dining room table. We gave her the short version of how miserable we were. When she asked us what she could do to help, I asked her if she could find Elly a place to live. She took Chanel upstairs and questioned her in private. Then, once she'd gone outside to her car, Elly stopped her in the driveway.

The FACS worker later asked Lee about my sexuality. As if my being gay had anything to do with the well-being of my children, or with Elly's affair. Lee responded to her by asking her just that. And yet again, during another so-called routine visit, she would ask him the same question, and he would answer her the same way.

My biggest problem with this woman, who was obviously prejudice, was that she didn't think anything was wrong with she and Elly having their initial discussion about me in front of Hunter. He later informed me that she had said she suspected I was gay. (Yeah, and I suspected she was a bitch—looks like we were both right.) She was lucky I complained to her personally on the phone, and didn't report her conduct to her superiors. Wish I had though. And there it was: the very thing that had kept me silent my entire life—ignorance!

Meanwhile, Mr.East continued to be Elly's best friend. He drove her to all of her treatments. Usually, if I wanted to know how she was doing, I had to call and ask him. When I found out from my mother that he'd been griping about my calls, I stopped. From then on, I was left in the dark in the matters of Elly's health. However, from what I could see, she was doing fine.

Her attacks on me kept getting worse, and always involved our children. I even had to set a curfew for Hunter's nights at the Serpentarium with his mother. She was bringing him home at one and two in the morning, including Sunday nights. I heard her yelling at him to get up for school, saying, "Get your ass out of bed!"

Many nights Hunter had to phone his friend's father to come and pick him up. I couldn't because Elly had our only car there. His friend's father later told me how he'd witnessed Elly being intoxicated. Hunter verified this when he told me his mother couldn't drive him home because she was sick from drinking too much. Elly became furious when I brought this to her attention, and accused me of trying to make her out to be an alcoholic.

At the peak of Hunter's interest in the Serpentarium, I was awoken at about 2AM one night by a knock at my door. My son was being dropped off by some kid affiliated with the Serpentarium. The minute Hunter stepped inside, I immediately noticed he was wavering. "Have you been *drinking*?" I asked him.

He was glowing when he said, "Mom let me sip from her beers."

Elly didn't come home at all that night.

Arguing soon ensued between Hunter and Elly. I suspect he began to dislike the relationship between his mother and her man, and Elly began to dislike her son's honesty. His habitual visits to the Serpentarium began to taper, as did his time spent with his mother. She'd taken over his hangout. No longer needing our son as her excuse for being there, Elly was more than happy to leave him behind.

During the four months of Elly's chemo treatments, she'd asked me to cut and style the wig my mother and sister's had paid for. I did so, no less than three times. I was a sucker, dolling her up for my Australian, snake-charming replacement. I had since lifted yet another brick from Elly's bag by telling Debbie and her two sons my secret. Debbie had raised her boys under strict Christian beliefs. The three of them were sweet enough in consoling the sinner that I am, but Debbie would never believe that I understood what I was claiming to be. She convinced herself that I was confused. I knew beforehand that she was not going to accept me for who I really was, and I accepted *that*.

When I finally told Elly what I'd been up to in sharing my truth with my family, she was furious.

"What the hell did you tell them for?" she yelled, while taking clothes out of the washing machine.

I was taken aback. I thought I'd been doing right by her. She didn't see it that way. That was the day she told me she couldn't stand my gayness. I wasn't exactly certain what that was supposed to mean. But for the days and weeks that followed, her words haunted me to no end. I would catch her watching me as I cut hair. I started to watch myself, wondering if I was waving my hands about and acting like a queer. Was that what she meant? I wondered.

I never believed that I gave any indication that I was gay. Not in my mannerisms, anyway. But now I was unsure about myself. She couldn't stand my 'gayness!' What gayness? I struggled with her words for weeks, until I saw Liam. I told him how fucked up she'd left me. That I couldn't work on hair without monitoring my gestures. I was angry as hell with her for having done this to me. Liam was so awesome. He reassured me that she was just trying to hurt me.

Why was it that after seventeen years of being married, she suddenly hated something about me that had always been? There were many things about me that should have given me away to everyone, but didn't. I think she was seeing what she wanted to see. I suppose she would have thought the way I tied my shoes was gay, or brushed my teeth, or *breathed*! That's what I told myself. That was how I got passed my self-censorship. I didn't waste another moment worrying about what Elly thought of me. Her opinion no longer mattered because it was fueled by hate. I was finally finished shifting the weight of my secret from her shoulders to the shoulders of others. Besides, I realized that I'd been carrying the bag of bricks the entire time, and it would always be mine to carry.

FUCK FORGIVENESS!

WE WERE PAST THE HALFWAY point of July. I'm not sure how I was able to stay on my feet and take care of my clients. Only a handful really knew what was happening in my house. I have a trained sense of humor and a smile to match. But even my sense of humor could not save me from the ultimate act of betrayal and hate that Elly was about to unleash. I should have known something was not right the moment it began, but it wouldn't have made a difference. I couldn't stop what was already in play.

Elly gathered the four kids and disappeared to her sister's house. One of the twins called me later that night to say they were having a sleepover. I sensed the oddity instantly. Elly had never done this before. Her sister's house was a pigsty. The two of us could never stand to visit for very long. Then out of the blue it's a sleepover. This came just after Elly's chemo treatments had concluded. Looking back at the way I was with her, I can't believe I allowed her to stay in our home, knowing she was with another man.

Their sleepover night turned into four days. I called Elly to ask her what was going on. She tried very hard to convince me it was all innocent. Come Friday morning, while I was clipping the hair of a married couple, there came a knock at my door. I excused myself to answer it. A lump rose into my throat at the sight of two police officers. When I opened the door, a lanky young woman stepped up.

"Michael Dube?" she asked.

"Yeah."

"This is for you," she said, grinning.

I knew at once that she was an acquaintance of Elly's from the Serpentarium. And just when I thought there were only female sharks in the water, Mr. East came walking up to my doorstep.

"Mr. East? What are **you** doing here?" I asked him. The smugness on his face and in his voice made my blood boil.

"I'm here to help my friend," he said.

And then I saw her: Elly, with her eyes strictly avoiding contact with mine as she approached.

"Just stand aside, Sir, and let her get her personal belongings," said the taller cop. His partner was short and heavy. Mr. East squeezed his way up the three steps into my kitchen entrance.

"Your friend?" I echoed. "She doesn't even like you, you moron."

The taller officer stood between myself, at the bottom of the steps, and Mr. East as he turned and hissed, "I put your father in the hospital. I can do the same to you."

The officer gently forced Mr. East back and said, "Just get what you came to get, Sir."

I moved up closer to Elly as she squirmed her way inside. "This is how you choose to do this?" I asked her.

"Yep," she snapped. "You left me no choice."

I followed her up into the kitchen but the officer stopped me, saying, "You'll have to wait here till they're done."

"No, I'm not," I said. "I have clients in there."

I no sooner returned to my clients, when my sisters Tammy and Bi arrived, followed by my mother—who was on fire! She started cussing at her husband in front of all of us. She told him he should have kept his nose out of it. And him, being the smug bastard that he is, stopped, turned to the officer, and said, "Can you please remove these people until we're done?"

My mother, had the officers not been there, would have laid a beating on him. Even I had to tell her to stop. But when Mr. East was heading back upstairs for his next grab, I called up to him, saying, "By the way, Mr. East, I'm *not* my father."

"No," he said, "he would have been easier."

"Such a smartass, aren't you?" I said.

He and Elly snatched as much as they could within about ten minutes. And that would be all she would ever take from our home.

The papers her friend had handed me were court documents, listing in Elly's handwriting, two or three pages of lies. Like how I was not supportive during her treatment period. As much bullshit as she'd dealt me up to that point, her written lies still shocked me. Everything was my fault, and I was horrible because I had admitted to the world to being gay.

That night I wished Mr. East dead, Elly dead, and I tried to drown myself in the tub; but I couldn't even do that. My bathwater must have been 50% tears. I think I'd convinced myself that I deserved my pain. I fucked up. I felt stripped of everything I loved. Having Mr. East involved only added vinegar to my wounds—*(Add salt or whatever you want to your wounds, I'm adding vinegar, dammit.)* When would that bastard get a taste of his own misery? When would he suffer? He'd been causing my family hurt for so many years. Where was *his* hurt? I wondered.

A one night sleepover turned into fifty-one days. FIFTY-ONE DAYS! Elly kept my children from seeing me or speaking to me for fifty-one days. She robbed me of them for fifty-one days. For fifty-one days I was insanely depressed. For fifty-one days I looked for my children's faces amongst my nieces and nephews. For fifty-one days she tortured me without reason. I will never forgive her for that. Fuck forgiveness!

During those fifty-one days, I was under so much duress. My dreams were poisoned by images of the life I once knew. I walked about with my teeth ground in anger. My chest ached, my throat was tight, and I was lost. I paid many visits to my trusted friend Liam. During which time I confessed to him about the sickness in my brain (the desire to kill myself and end it all). He reminded me about the ones who'd be left behind to suffer. I remember being unable to stop myself from crying. He'd even left me alone in his office for about thirty minutes, just to cry.

"Mike," he told me, "I'm not putting any of this in your file because you'd never get your kids back. You have to promise me you won't do anything to hurt yourself."

I knew he was right about the kids, so I promised, even though I wasn't sure I could keep that promise.

"I don't want to admit you into the hospital. Are you going to be okay?" he asked me.

I nodded.

"I have a lot invested in you, Mike. You can't do this to me. If you killed yourself, I would never forget you, but I would never forgive you."

Liam hugged me and told me he wanted me to return to see him the next week. I knew this was his way of getting me through my pain, making promises to be alive. The more I thought of my children, the more I knew I had to fight these urges until they no longer had a hold of me. It was a dreadful time.

Around the same period, Brian had suddenly stopped returning my calls. I couldn't understand it. I needed as many friends as I could get. The slightest neglect I felt from people was more than I could bear—I was fragile. I thought I'd always been good to Brian, but when he finally did call me back, I learned just how pathetic I'd been.

He told me he felt uncomfortable with me. It wasn't my depression, it was the comparisons I kept making of him to Liam. I guess he felt like a second, not as good, version of Liam. He was right, partly, and partly he was wrong. It didn't help that Elly had told the kids he was my boyfriend. Either way, I begged him to remain friends with me, but to no avail. He wasn't the friend I'd thought he was. To abandon me in the middle of all I was experiencing; he was not the friend I needed, but that didn't make it any easier for me to let go.

After losing Brian's friendship, I desperately needed to get myself out of Welland for a few days. My mind was on the verge of exploding. The one person who'd always been strong for me, who'd never belittled our relationship, was Dwayne. On a Friday I drove up to Delhi to spend the weekend with him. Within the first hour of being in Dwayne's company, I was already feeling better. Come Saturday night, however, I received a call from my son. He was home—at my home!

I listened to him describe the nightmare he and my daughters were dealing with living at Mona's house. He told me no one knew he had left. He was sick of his mother and sick of the lies. He wanted to be with me. Then he told me I should return right away; his mother was planning to invade my house the next morning with a bunch of guys. At 11o'clock that night, I said goodbye to my dearest friend and brother, and drove home.

Thanks to Hunter alerting me to her intentions, I was able to phone the police and stop Elly's raid before it happened. Elly was informed that she had no legal right to enter my home, having already collected her personal belongings. She would have to wait until we settled through the courts. I was so thankful to have my son back, and back for good. How ironic: the only child Elly spent any time with during the past year would be the first to abandon her wicked ways.

Probably too young to fully understand, I let Hunter know that he'd rescued his dad. His coming home had placed me back in the position of fatherhood. I was no longer alone. His presence gave me reason to live again. The sickness was not gone, but now I had my son to add to my ammunition against the invisible beast.

On A Bright, Sunny Day…

Try as I might, there was no way and no one to help me see my children. It seemed Elly had all the rights and I had none. People kept telling me I had rights, but if I did, they never saw the light of day. I tried the police. I tried FACS. Not even my lawyer could get me to see my kids. It wasn't until September, when school commenced, that Elly's game was finished.

A week before the start of school, I phoned the Principal and explained what had happened. She was already well acquainted with Elly's temper and treatment of the kids from the prior year, especially after an incident involving Hunter. I informed her that there was no court order in effect, and asked her if I could come to the school and see my baby girl. She was happy to oblige me.

(I have to break here to express just how torn I remain over my reunion with my darling Chanel. I knew how I felt as a child when Bi and I were reunited with Mom. This time, I was in Mom's shoes.)

I waited till about the third day of school. Elly had even tried to send Chanel to another school, on her own yet. Chanel must have freaked out or she wouldn't have put her back with the twins at her regular school. I sat in the Principal's office in tears as I told her what Elly had been up to. She had me wait in the cafeteria, across from the secretary's office. When Chanel came to the office, she turned and spotted me right away. She was in shock.

"Dad?" she said in her elfish voice.

"Hi, Chanel," I said, and got down on my knees to hug her, crying.

The secretary and the Principal were watching us from each side of the hallway. I remember feeling a great rush of rage through my body because Elly had forced us into this situation. I couldn't believe the legal powers that be ignored my every call for help, and left us to suffer at the hands of someone who'd obviously lost touch with all things humane. My own lawyer was happy to tell me to wait for school to start to see my kids—useless.

There was only one man who tried to tell Elly that what she was doing to myself and the kids was wrong, and that man was Liam. He'd spent hours watching me fall apart in his office. Hearing me blame myself for everything horrible that was happening. Convincing me how wrong I was. Confirming how wrong Elly was. Keeping me alive! Although I told him in letters, I don't really think he knows how powerful of a 'friend' he was—and is—to me.

I mention Liam a lot because he literally did keep me alive and well. Many times I've had my feelings hurt by him, but that's because I'm a big sensitive sap—give a queer a break. His goodness far exceeds his weak points. He kept me going long enough to find a drawing in Chanel's backpack one day. The artwork depicted she and I and the day we were reunited in the school hallway. It at once warmed my heart and broke it. I framed that drawing to remind us both how much we love each other. *(Now I need to cry for a minute.)*

Locked Out Of The Pearly Gates

I turned thirty-nine in October of 2007. I was living the worst year of my life. Hunter and I were alone in the house. He was twelve. I wasn't strong yet, in fact, I felt weaker than ever. The court date had been postponed, but at least a visitation order had been issued. I was allowed to see the girls every other weekend, plus Tuesdays overnight, and Thursdays till 7:30PM—half of the month. It wasn't enough. Not for me and not for Chanel. On her weekends with the girls, Elly didn't even stay home. She'd leave the twins to watch Chanel while she went to her boyfriend's.

Without fail, I would receive countless phone calls from Chanel. She would cry to me, begging for me to come and pick her up. She once told me she was crying while looking at a photograph of she and I. She said she missed me. Her longing to live with me never went away. The calls were so heart-breaking. She didn't cry like a child who'd been scolded; she wept softly like a person filled with sorrow. All I could think about was why Elly couldn't see what she was doing to our daughter. I suspect she was too busy thinking about what she was putting *me* through.

Meanwhile, the type of depression I had experienced when we were working in the salon was nothing like the one I was battling now. There were no highs, only lows and extreme lows. My memory was poor, my headaches constant, my heart beats erratic, and I was crying every day as if it were as natural as blinking. The hours of crying uncontrollably and plotting my death were like having seizures of the mind. When I snapped out of the 'seizures,' I felt utterly drained. I went on in this way for quite some time. In fact, honestly, I can't say I'm better yet. Suicide isn't an option, but sadness continues to leave me broken.

It's not a wonder that I'm not well. I didn't have my children with me for Christmas of 2007. Elly had them for Christmas, for Easter, and even for Father's day, both in 2007 and 2008. For the second year in a row, my kids will be riding on the back of her boyfriend's float in the city parade. I don't attend. Watching Elly wave to the crowds from her seat in his truck is more than I can stomach.

Elly isn't the only one causing me grief. I face loved ones every day who still don't want to accept me for me. Liam had a difficult time convincing me to accept myself and be proud of who I was. "You need to go out and have fun. You need to meet people and have an affair of your own!" he said.

I wanted to, but I really didn't know how. I didn't know how to live life as a queer. I'd never done it before. I was used to being with Elly and the kids. Used to staying home and being a family man. How does a 39-year-old man go about beginning a new life, living as a queer? It wasn't as simple as just going out to a bar and flirt with other guys. I told Liam I wasn't the slut type; I was the long-term relationship type. It wasn't going to be easy to lose Michael Pichael—as my sister Debbie had nicknamed me when I was a kid—and rediscover Michael.

With Mom amongst those who were having a difficult time understanding me, I was taking two steps forward and three steps back. As recent as April, while I was coloring Mom's hair, she sweetly said to me, "What you need is to find a good woman to take care of you."

My jaw hit the floor. Was she not listening when I told her I was gay? I couldn't help feeling angry. I nearly let it go without saying anything, but as I rinsed her hair, I felt I *had* to say something, so I said: "Mom, no matter how much you may wish it, it's never going to happen. I'm never going to be with another woman. I may never be with a man, but I'll never be with another woman. I'm sorry, but that's just the way it is."

She apologized. I wrote it off as a slip of the tongue, but I know it wasn't. Damn us queers for being so disgusting to the world in our needs. All those poor mothers and fathers who'll never grasp the concept of homosexuality. Why my child? Why my son? They must ask themselves every night and day. Well, this may surprise you, but I've been asking myself WHY my entire life! If being gay really was a choice, I would have chose to be straight. Now I choose to be happy. It's just not as easy as it sounds.

You know, April did start off calm enough. I was seeing my three girls, as per the court order. Hunter had proven himself a great son over and over again. He's not afraid to tell me he loves me. He helped me out around the house when I asked him to. He'd even begun to do his own laundry, folding included! He and I got along just fine. We actually had quite a bit in common. His only real problem was his hatred of the school system. He's a little too stubborn for his teachers' liking. For all the rest that he is, I can handle his distaste for educational figures.

As for me, I'd taken my first step toward bettering myself for the future. Liam had inspired me to become a counselor. So I applied at our city college for the Social Service Worker Program. Applying was a rather ridiculous three step procedure. First of all, before I could even go any further in the process, I had to dish out eighty-nine dollars. This I was lucky to have left in my bank account from my income tax return.

Then I was given instructions on what I had to submit for their approval. A resume, a letter of recommendation, and a 750 word essay describing why I wanted to take the course, and what qualifications I thought I had. The resume was easy. The letter of recommendation I got from Liam, of course. And the essay, well, we all know I like to write. Within three days of submitting my proposal, I received a letter stating what number on their waiting list I was. At least I was on the list.

I was feeling pretty confident I'd made the right choice in choosing the S.S.W.P. There was now something in my future I had to look forward to. That moment of gratification was just that—a moment. For all her good intentions, Debbie had once again caused grief to ring my telephone.

It began with a few nude calendar girl pictures on Hunter's bedroom wall. The models were in nonsexual poses, without their vaginas showing. Big fucking deal. I made a huge error in judgment when I let Debbie see those pictures.

"You let your son have pictures of naked women?" she said, flustered.

"Let him?" I chortled. "I bought the calendar for him," I said, matter of fact.

She made a comment about Hunter becoming insensitive to woman later in life, and seeing them only as objects. Of course, I thought that was completely absurd. I was soon to learn that she was so appalled by it all, she complained to Mom, Bi, my niece, and my father's youngest brother. If that had been the end of it, I wouldn't have cared, but it wasn't.

Debbie came over again shortly thereafter. I made another error, when I expressed my anger toward religion and God. Feeling like she needed to pray for her brother, Debbie went to see Dad's youngest brother's wife—yes, I am leaving them nameless. From that point everything exploded at their end. Deb came back to see me to tell me that one of our relatives had spilled my beans to my grandmother. I still don't know who it was, but that person is a dick.

I then telephoned my uncle to ask him who it was that thought it necessary to out me to my 88-year-old grandmother, whom I've always been close to and love dearly. He wouldn't tell me, but he did take it upon himself to lecture me on the evils of my parenting skills and my homosexuality. Amidst the storm of depression and loss I'd been under, my wonderful uncle preached to me.

"Do you think you're doing your son any favors by letting him have those on his walls? How would you like it if those were your daughters up there?" he rambled on.

I shook my head in disbelief. *Get a grip*, I thought. Before I could defend myself, he dropped the topic about naked pictures and dove right into my personal life. He said he would tell his mother on me. My 50-something-year-old uncle was going to tell his mommy on me. I couldn't believe what I was listening to. He said if I *chose* to live my life that way, he could not have anything to do with me. That in his eyes and the eyes of God, I was disgusting.

He told me the Bible clearly states that there is no place in Heaven for homosexuals. He advised me to live the rest of my life alone, if I didn't want another woman.

I interrupted him at that point, and said, "I'm thirty-nine and you think I'm gonna spend the rest of my life alone, living in celibacy? I'm not a priest."

"If you make that choice, I can't speak to you anymore. Don't blame me for it, it's your own doing," he said.

Funny thing is: I had just recently told his eldest son during his haircut that he had two wonderful parents. Now I don't exist to them. I imagine I won't exist to many people soon. Can't say I wasn't sore at Debbie, but I'm over it. At one time, I thought religion was a good thing for her, but now I believe it's what makes her so ill. Poor Debbie wants to save all the world and her siblings from hell. I guess she sees me as another sinner on his hurried way to the furnace. No matter. I love my Debbie-Webbie!

She did apologize to me for the uncle situation. I know she hadn't foreseen him reacting like such an ignorant ass. This same uncle had been coming to me for his haircuts as well. On three or four occasions, he'd offered me the opportunity of having Mr. East 'taken care of.'

"It may not be someone you know, or even I know. But you say the word and I'll take care of it," he told me.

I'm not sure exactly what he meant by 'taken care of,' but one can assume there would be some suffering involved. That kind of offer from the same man who believes *I'm* a vile sinner. He'll probably deny he ever said those things to me, but if he does believe in God, as he claims, than he knows he can't lie to his God.

After hearing how upset I was about our uncle's call, Bi decided to call him herself. He told her he was going to warn his two sons to stay clear of me because he didn't want them to catch whatever disease I might have. (What…an…Ass.) Now there is stupidity at its best. He asked Bi that if there was nothing wrong with what I am, then why is it a secret? To answer his question: It is because of ignorant people just like you!

People would love it if all queers would remain in the closet. I still hide from clients whom I know would drop me in a heartbeat if they knew. Not that my skills would be different, but I would be different. It's a shame. A shame that they torture me without even knowing they are.

On the flipside of things, there's Dad. Since my uncle claimed he was going to expose me to the fucking planet, I thought it best that I reach Dad before he did. Now you must understand, I never intended to tell my father because he's pretty frail these days. Diabetes and a number of strokes aged him about fifteen years. I wanted to leave him alone. I didn't see the need to break his heart, having already lost his first son. I didn't want to disappoint him. I'm not certain why, but telling him I was gay was the most difficult thing I'd ever had to do.

"Dad," I said on the phone. "I have something I want to tell you." I was already sobbing like a baby. This was Dad. My Dad. The man who used to sing "Michael Row Your Boat Ashore" when I was little. The man who used to wink at me at the dinner table, and I would blink both eyes trying to wink back. The man I'd finally reconnected with while living up north with him. This was him—Dad. Why had his brother done this to me—to us? He had no right.

"What is it, Mike?" Dad asked me, now weeping at the other end. Following all his sufferings, Dad wept on a daily basis. I'm sure the sound of my pain had instantly triggered his tears.

"I didn't want to tell you," I said.

"Tell me what, Mike? What is it?"

"I don't want you to hate me," I said, panting in tears.

"No matter what it is, I would never hate you."

"Your brother said he was going to tell you, that's why I'm telling you. I didn't want to tell you," I went on.

"It's okay, Mike. I'm here for you. I love you," Dad said.

"Dad…I'm gay," I finally whispered.

And that's when his voice changed. He didn't sound sad or angry, he sounded surprised. Not the kind of *shock* surprised, but more like *that's it, that's your big secret*, surprised.

"So what?" he said. "You can't help what you are. You're still my son and I'm still your dad. I'll always love you, Son."

"Thanks, Dad. I love you too."

That was it. The man I knew was a great man did not let me down. I felt as though I'd been blinded by years of horrible happenings, and with one phone call, I realized I was still part of the same remarkable, loving—EVER loving family. I was not let down. I also realized that since I had the love and acceptance of my family, no one else's opinion in this entire universe mattered!

Heaven's Not For Me

My phone was ringing off the hook all through April, with creditors hassling me for money I did not have. Although I wasn't picking up, their messages on my answering machine were enough to make me come unhinged. I only spoke to a couple of them. I even wept during one call in which I made the poor guy feel so bad for me, he changed his tone from angry to apologetic. I have a feeling if it was up to him, he would have let me off the hook.

Lee caught me crying after that call. I was so embarrassed, but at the same time I didn't care. I was beaten. I couldn't take anymore. Elly may have been the one with the disease, but I was the martyr. Against Bi's advice, I filed for bankruptcy for the second time. I didn't see any other way out. It was impossible for me to come up with all the payments the five credit card companies wanted from me (yes, you read that correctly—five!)

Part of my depression is that I tend to shop. During Elly's treatments I shopped and shopped and shopped. I'm not alone. Bi and Bev are the same way. You'd think we could help ourselves, but it's not that simple. Mostly I was purchasing furniture and crap for our salon. Elly would have benefited from my illness had she not chosen to abandon our life together.

May rolled around and might as well have rolled right over me for all its bullshit. Liam had promised to take me with him to Toronto for a night out. Do I have to bother telling you he stood me up? Little did he realize that for all his lifting me up in his office, he was burying me deeper and deeper with his broken promises. I didn't understand him. You'd think a doctor would stay true to his word, or at least call me when he knew he wasn't going to bring me along. He never did. Now I know why physicians say 'call me in the morning, ' (because they will never call you!)

To add to my *happiness*, my lawyer's moronic secretary called me to let me know that the June court date I'd been anxiously awaiting had been shoved back to September. I was enraged. How long do people think an eight-year-old can live in torment? I know they don't give a shit because if they did, Chanel would have never been left with her mother. Elly's neglect and all her bullshit didn't seem to count for anything. Let's just automatically hand the children over to their mother because she's their mother. Just because my children didn't drop out of my ass doesn't make them any less mine. Do I sound angry? Fuck yeah, I'm angry.

"What are you guys doing, waiting until Chanel becomes of age and then we won't need the court?" I asked my lawyer's secretary.

"It's not us. It's the court system," she said. "You might want to try calling your local M.P."

Yeah, that's their answer for everything—call someone else!

In the meantime, Elly and her mother continued to degrade me in front of the twins. Taylor and Randee were at my house one weekend and filled me in on all the good stuff they had to bear. Never have I had to ask the girls about anything, they are the ones so bothered by their grandma and mother's ignorance, they come to me and share their feelings.

Taylor told me how Elly's mother continues to make gay slurs about me to them. When Randee told Elly she was thinking of moving back in with me, Elly told her if she did, she'd never see her again. The twins also told me that their mother had a strange name listed on her phone. Not understanding who it could be, they dialed the number and were surprised to reach *my* answering machine. My number was under the name 'Jerk.'

That same weekend, my cousin came for a haircut. My cousin just happens to be my uncle's son. (Yeah, you know, *that* uncle.) I wish I would have recorded his son to one day play back what he'd said to me, so he could hear how asinine he sounded. On one hand, he was telling me my sex life was none of his business; on the other hand, he actually said that if he ever came for a cut and I had a partner there, he would leave. He went on to tell me how he thinks homosexuality is the most repulsive thing *ever*! Being in real state, he once had to deal with a gay couple. Well, actually, according to him, he didn't deal with them at all. He said he found them so foul that he passed their case on to another agent. I can't imagine what shameful thing they must have done in front of him. Let me see: smile at one another?

So, I'm standing there, cutting his hair, listening to his hate talk, and I was supposed to accept it with a grin. Being the gentle person that I am, I let him pay me for the last cut I would ever give him, or anyone from his family. For all of God's people that I've known, they were all full of hate. Well, God can have them, and they can have Him. If my soul has to hang around for eternity with a bunch of hateful souls, count me out. After a lifetime of devotion, perhaps Heaven is not for me.

JUST END IT SYNDROME

ON MAY 30TH, the notice I'd been expecting was finally hand-delivered to my doorstep. Ironically, the deliverer was undoubtedly gay. I was given nine days to remove myself from my home. I had known this letter was soon to come, but when it did, its impact was no less devastating. My family kept asking me what I was going to do, where I was going to go. I didn't know.

There I was with nine days to pack up an entire household of belongings and move Hunter and myself out. I telephoned Niagara Housing and told them what was happening. I told the woman on the phone that my son and I were truly going to be living in a box on the street. She didn't seem too disconcerted. No one cares. Her advice was for us to move in with family or friends until a house came up for us. A wait that could take years.

My next call was to Dad. I cried as I explained the notice to him. He was upset for me, and opened his house to us. The problem was I no longer had a vehicle. My car had broken down permanently. I was feeling it again—complete loss. No wife, no daughters, no car, no house, and no life. I fell into a familiar condition I called the 'just end it syndrome,' where all I wanted for myself was for life to end.

I was hoping Liam could lift my spirits the way he always seemed to, but no such guidance would come. Not one, but two appointments in a row were cancelled with him. His cancer-stricken father was taking him away from work. He had to bring his father up to Hamilton. To make matters worse, I had run out of Paxil. Talk about withdrawal symptoms. I was so dizzy, I could barely open my eyes. Every attempt I made to attain more medication failed. Liam's new secretary just kept telling me she couldn't help me. No matter how desperate I tried, I was left to suffer through it. The very same week, when I should have been busy packing for our move, I was bedridden. I had to cancel all of my hair appointments.

By the third day the spell had consumed me; I was immobilized. If I'd had an ounce of strength left, I might have considered suicide. In fact, I did consider it, but I couldn't do it. Hunter was still with me. My beautiful son was my life-line. Besides, the way my palpitations were assaulting me from within, I was under the impression that suicide was not going to be necessary.

That night I managed to crawl into the bath, but it didn't do me any good. I soaked myself for about two hours, bawling harder than I'd ever bawled before. I completely drained myself. I felt as if I'd collapsed inside, as if all my worth was gone, as if there couldn't possibly be a tomorrow. I could hear myself crying above the radio, and I couldn't stop. Just like the crashing of my life, I couldn't stop it. How could I be a dad? How could I take care of Hunter, when I couldn't seem to take care of myself?

Lying there in that tub, gazing up at the walls, I couldn't believe I was being forced to leave my house. I had no control over any part of my life (the world was controlling me!) Liam alone could have spared me the pain of withdrawals. Elly could have made different choices and spared us all from losing our home. My friend, Brian, could have chosen to remain a friend and spared me his rejection. My uncle could have chosen to be a little more understanding and a little less punishing. Debbie could have chosen to support me instead of condemning me. My brother could have chosen to tell me he was planning to move before he made the decision to. I would have tried to convince him to stay. And dammit, why did I make the choice to come out? I could have stayed in the closet as I had all those years. I could have kept my fucking mouth shut. I could have been ***normal***!

I soaked…and I cried.

Moving On

By the time Liam returned to his office, he was bogged down with patients. I didn't bother to make an appointment to see him, but I did call to refill my prescription once and for all. Knowing how little time I had left in my house—days—I was taking three pills a day instead of the recommended dosage of ONE. I had to do something to rid myself of the dizziness. How else would I be able to move.

Tammy had just moved into her new house on the previous weekend, so she stopped by to bring us some boxes. Debbie also brought a few boxes. My little Hunter had already begun to pack. He'd cleaned out the entire spare room and was working on getting his room done. I could hear him bustling about below me the entire time I was laid up.

By Friday Randee, Taylor, and Chanel came over for their weekend with me. Still a little dizzy and very week, I did my best to begin the task of packing everything up to move. There I was, my final weekend in my house, and I still didn't know where I was going to be moving to! Then I received a call from Bev. She told Hunter and I we were welcome to stay with her until a house was found for us.

For three days straight, with the use of Steve's pickup (Bi's husband) myself and my three older kids packed and moved all of our belongings into Bev's barn. Unless you've experienced something similar, you have no idea how it feels to see your house crammed into an old barn. I had to force myself not to worry about things being damaged or lost. Like everything else it was out of my hands.

I was so proud of my children. They worked their butts off. If not for them, I would have been at a loss for help. It was an exhausting three days. I took what I could with me. I had even stripped my garden for every plant I had planted the years before and refused to leave behind. The biggest problem I faced now was how to continue with my business of cutting hair, when I was no longer in Welland. (Bev's farm sits on a remote road in Port Colborne.) Even if I wanted to visit each client at their homes, I couldn't because I had no car.

Bev allowed me to have my salon chair set up in her large kitchen, but it wouldn't do me any good if my clients were unwilling to drive out. By the end of that weekend, I was glad to be rid of my connection to the only house Elly and I had ever owned together. Hunter and I were free to make a clean start, if only we could make a start. This was about as low as I could be. I phoned Niagara Housing again and told them how my new location was interfering with my visitations with my girls. I was told the same thing as last time: you'll just have to wait.

Bev was generous in giving Hunter and I a place to stay, but things were far from well. The kids and I would have to sleep on mattresses on the floor, and I knew our presence was taxing for Bev. Another slave to the power of stress, every little detail was making her nuts. From the kids leaving glasses on her counters, to simply having too many people in her house, Bev was seeing red, and that was only the first weekend!

I changed my mailing address to Bev's at the post office, but my mail continued to get dropped off at my house. One such letter I picked up there had come from Niagara College. I opened it to discover that my acceptance into the Social Service Worker Program had been approved for January of 2009. That was the start date I had hoped for. I couldn't believe it, something positive had come my way.

So many aspects of my life remained unresolved. Custody for Chanel is my top priority. Once Hunter and I are given a house to live in, then we will feel like we can finally move on. But as long as we're here at Bev's, neither of us will be comfortable or at peace. As of now, there just isn't any real sense of closure. I'm still lonely. I still have no car, no home, or access to my clients, no companion, and not much in the way of hope. It's a fucked up place I am in right now.

When you're down, people like to tell you that everything will work out and you'll be fine, *better* than you were before. I keep waiting for them to be proven right. I'm still sick from stress and people have me running around for all sorts of papers to satisfy themselves on whether or not I am needy. Legal Aid wants this list of papers, welfare wants that list, and the bankrupt company wants their list of crap. Companies and people whose jobs it is to help you seem to have no concept of what help means. They sit behind their desks and fill in the blanks on their computers, but your heartaches are unimaginable to them. You're just another file to add to the shelf. So many times, as I sat in their uncomfortable chairs while they sat in their luxurious leather office seats, did I feel certain they hadn't the slightest idea of who I was, or what I'd been through. I hope I never present myself as being imperceptive in the eyes of someone I'm trying to help.

There are those whom I will forever hide myself from…just because. Take my wonderful loving grandmother, for instance. She recently sent my mother a card and letter to wish her a happy birthday. In her letter, Grandma told Mom not to worry about me because this whole homosexual thing is "all in my head." When Mom told me about it, I think she finally realized herself how silly 'all in your head' really sounded. After all, Mom had been told by Mr. East a few years back that *her* depression was 'all in her head.' (Oh yeah, and Mom's back with him again.) The difference this time is that her children are not back with him. We gave up forgiving the unforgivable.

My twin daughters are graduating from grade eight tomorrow. I'll have to face their mother and perhaps their grandmother, too. I'm so stressed these days, I still have dizzy bouts. Every time I have to see my possessions piled up in Bev's barn, gathering shit from the swallows, it makes me feel hopeless—defeated. The shit just keeps piling higher and higher in my life. (And me without a shovel!)

EPILOGUE * JULY 2010

My original intention was to write a part two for this book, filled from front to back cover with all the wonderful events that would have transpired. *Right.* As time went on, it became painfully clear that good fortune was not yet ready to make my acquaintance. So, here now, in its shortest version, is a rundown of the crap that followed the other crap!

When I finally moved out of Bev's house, it was to occupy a tiny basement apartment back in Welland, a couple blocks from Mom's house. And when I say 'tiny', I mean tiny (kitchen, bathroom, living room, and one bedroom). Notice the amount of bedrooms I listed—ONE! Hunter and I both slept on the living room floor, not having any beds at that time, or living room furniture, either. Eventually, I set up two beds in the single bedroom for the twins to sleep in.

Then the bullshit.

Niagara Housing was happy with my new living arrangement. They apparently saw nothing wrong with a father and son and three daughters sharing a one bedroom apartment the size of most people's kitchens. There were only two windows in the place, and since they were at ground level, with a fence just outside the windows, we had no view, no light, no life. Once again I became bedridden with dizziness and palpitations that I thought would cancel my ticket. Mom was stressing out over my health and adding to my own stress, as I did not want to make her sick.

Then I was informed that I would have to stand before a committee of Niagara Housing fools and explain why I felt I deserved to remain on their list for a geared-to-income place. Are you getting how absurd this all was? One week before my so-called meeting, a call about an apartment in one of their co-op buildings came through. Needless to say, I desperately wanted it—needed it. And the place is mine, I'm told, as long as I can get someone to co-sign for me. No problem, I thought, Tammy signed last time, so I'll just ask her to sign again.

Well, I asked, and she refused. Yep, my only sibling that could rescue my kids and I from the basement nightmare refused to lend her signature, cause you know, of course, I most certainly would fuck things up and she'd be left having to pay my rent, right. (As if.) Was I upset? You have no idea. At that same time, Tammy's hubby was using my piece of shit car that my uncle had unloaded on me. It wasn't insured, safetied, e-tested, or road-worthy, but he was already driving it back and forth to work. The only reason it was in their possession was because they told me to park it at their house for safe-keepings. So when Tammy refused her signature, I picked up my piece of shit car, dead in her driveway. Mom and I had to drive to Bev's for booster cables, drive back to Tammy's, and the entire time she was home and wouldn't answer her door. I traded that car for a better one, but the point of the story is that Tammy hasn't spoken to her evil, evil brother since (me), and it's been two years! I was devastated over it. I had nightmares over it. She'd broken my heart. I couldn't believe she could be so cruel, so cold and indifferent. I even tried to make up with her over the phone, but she said, "Don't ever call me again." Her only daughter had a baby boy, and my first glimpse of him at so many months old, was in a photograph at Bi's.

"Whose cute kid is this?" I'd asked Steve, Bi's hubby.

He chuckled, a little surprised by my ignorance, and said, "That's your nephew. Jenny's kid."

So now I only have two words for my loving sister Tammy—Happy Birthday!

Wow. That was the short version? As short as I could make it. Next on the shit list. Hmm. Let's see. Oh yeah. The day we moved into the new apartment, on the freaking third floor of the building, with me still dizzy and feeling oh-so-fucking-great, welfare fucked up with my check. They just didn't send one! The building attendants wouldn't let me have the key to the apartment until I paid upfront. I had to borrow the cash from Steve, then deal with more stalling and bullshit from the two bitches who worked the front desk at the welfare office. Who are those people? I mean, really. I think they're hired on their bitch status alone.

There I was with four kids and a truck loaded with all of our belongings, and they couldn't give a rat's ass. Oh yeah, nearly forgot to mention, the kids **ALL** moved in with me on that May 1, 2009. I was happier about that than a man who'd just won the lottery. They were my lottery. Here it is, by the way, June 28, 2010, and the kids are all still with me. But if I continue along that thought, I'll be skipping the other bullshit stuff, so just hold on.

Okay, so the next big issue I had to deal with was my stupid ex wife keeping the child tax benefit to herself. Here the kids and I were struggling with bills, clothing, and rationing our food, while the idiot lived like a queen. It would take SEVEN months before the morons who handle the child tax would get it through their thick skulls that I had all four children living with me now, and that Elly was breaking the law, while starving her own kids. Now she owes them five-thousand dollars (she told me herself).

With the back-pay the government now owed me and the kids, I was able to buy a used car, a living room set, beddings, dishes, clothes, FOOD, and give the kids a descent Christmas in 2009. During this past year, Elly never called here for the kids, never bothered with them, or Chanel. The only time she's with them is when *they* make a point of going to her. She's undeniably become an alcoholic, which she says isn't true since alcoholics must get drunk to be classified as such. H*ell*O!

These past few weeks have been quite stressful and depressing for me because she's been involving Chanel in her stupidity. She allowed Chanel (now 10-years-old) to drink from her vodka cooler one weekend, and the next I had to drive across town to pick Chanel up at Mona's house because Elly was too drunk to drive her home at 1:00AM! No, Elly, you don't have to be drunk every day to be an alcoholic, but you're doing a pretty good job of it.

On a good note, thanks to my incredible doctor's dedication

and love, I was finally placed on the Ontario Disability Support Program. After much trial and error, we'd found a handful of medications to keep my blood pressure under control, deal with my anxiety and depression, minimize my body pain, treat my acid reflux, and… Okay, maybe the meds don't work miracles, but my health has most definitely improved. Heck, I don't even think about suicide as much. I've even had a few sexual encounters that weren't all that disgusting.

My bankruptcy payments came to an end, and none too soon for my wallet. Just recently received the discharge certificate. I pretty much retired from hairstyling, as my hands, wrists, arms, back, legs…all of it hurts too much. I don't think anyone truly understands what I live with. The kids know I nap quite a lot. I try to be as lively as I can but it's not always a choice. Elly filed for a divorce, as expected. Oh man, and she made a complete fool of herself at the meeting with our lawyers and the children's lawyer. I won't go into detail, but let's just say I walked out of that meeting feeling *really* good. Everything I had been telling the lawyers about her, she proved right.

Not long ago I bumped into my lawyer at the court house. I told him what was happening that brought me there, and also that the kids were all under my care now. He smiled slyly from ear to ear and said, "I knew I had the better client. Good for you, Mike." In this past year alone I self-published two books of poetry. I'm currently taking a moment's break from finishing my horror/thriller novel for self-publication. It's not about fame and fortune for me, obviously. It's about sharing my work with my family, friends, and especially my kids. Being a man of humble stance, this is the best of me that I can offer them. I want them to know their Dad as more than their Dad, but as a human being. I hold no secrets… except for the true identity of my ex and her family.

And I hereby state that everything I have written in this book is the truth as I know it. Who knows, maybe love will still find me before I toss it all in. The twins turned sixteen in May, while Hunter turned fifteen. The kids have all been amazing to me. Elly has no clue what she's thrown away. I love them ferociously and would never give them up again—NEVER!

And just in case you thought the bullshit was over, my rent is to increase July 1, 2010, but my check stub from ODSP hasn't increased. I notified them on May 3rd of the change. Guess it wasn't enough of a notice. Am I stressed? Naaahh……HELL YES! And a lingering debt from mine and Elly's house is still beckoning us; however, Elly isn't taking it seriously because my sister Bi was our co-signer, so she just assume let them harass her. My hands are tied in the situation—I'm poor. Dammit, where's a fucking miracle when you need one.

Yeah, and my great future in counseling didn't get off the ground. Turned out that because I'd filed for bankruptcy again, I wasn't entitled to collect student grants or loans. I never made it into the course because of it. I knew it was too good to be true. Truly there comes no relief in the life of someone like me. I get what I get, and that's all I get. No more, sometimes less, but no more.

In closing, I won't say a second book is not in the future, especially since I like to ramble on. Perhaps it won't be about my shitty life, and that way good things will be written. Who am I kidding, you people thrive on the sufferings of others. I can insult you now that you've come to the end of my book. I'm joking. But my advise to anyone who isn't as wealthy as the Hiltons, don't get caught without a shovel, 'cause there's a lot of B.S!

In the words of Donny and Mary:

Good Night, Everybody!

Made in United States
Cleveland, OH
04 November 2026

47642856R00107